LOSER MAKES GOOD

Also Available from University of Hell Press:

by Eirean Bradley
the I in team

by Greg Gerding
The Burning Album of Lame
Venue Voyeurisms: Bars of San Diego
Loser Makes Good: Selected Poems 1994
Piss Artist: Selected Poems 1995-1999
The Idiot Parade: Selected Poems 2000-2005

Forthcoming from University of Hell Press:

by Greg Gerding
I'll Show You Mine: People Talk Candidly About
    Love, Sex, and Intimacy
Song Stories (for the Wrecked)
Venue Voyeurisms: Strip Clubs of Portland

by Dee Madden
The Mimeograph Project

Loser Makes Good
(Selected Poems 1994)

by Greg Gerding

Illustrations by McHank

This book published by University of Hell Press.
www.universityofhellpress.com

© 2008 Greg Gerding

Book Design by Vince Norris
www.norrisportfolio.com

Illustrations and Cover by McHank
www.McHank.com

This book is a Special Edition printing with brand new variant cover and illustrations by McHank, and all content "remastered" by the author in © 2012.

All rights reserved. No part of this book may be reproduced or transmitted in any form or by any means, electronic or mechanical, including photocopying, recording or by any information storage and retrieval system, without written permission from the author, except for the inclusion of brief quotations in a review.

Published in the United States of America.
ISBN 978-1-938753-00-8

Table of Contents

Introduction

Blank Book One (January – February)

Tabula Rasa	19
Bad Dream #1182 (Cats vs. Cars)	20
Those Moments That Lie Just Beyond	22
Broadway-Bound Love	24
Lewisburg Prison	26
Imagining Suicide	28
Homeless Mail Veteran	30
Five Cigarettes and a Pen (Medium Point Bic Round Stic)	31
Guilt and the Senseless Stairmaster	33
A Cool and Peaceful Medium	34
A Couple of Hours Later	38
A Couple More Hours Later	40
A Wise Man Moved Slowly Past My Bench One Day	41
Have You Ever Seen Anything As Silly?	43
Spaghetti before Sex	44
Creatures of the World, Unite! (Hit Those Little Motherfuckers)	45
Poor Little Jimmy	47
Bored with Myself	49
Petty Fears and Philosophies Expressed at a Bare Bar Between a Middle Easterner and an American Who Just Won't Go Very Far	50
Planning For Your Birth	52
Common Sense	53

Blank Book Two (February – March)

Frogs in Tysons Corner, Virginia 57
Grill Me a Slice of Change and Hold the Onions 60
I Am Not Complaining... 62
Daydream #133,880 (I Often Picture Women Naked) 64
A Six-Pack and Who Gives a Flying Fuck 66
My Refuge Up Above It All... 67
You Have Got to Have a Sense of Humor 69
Squeeze It for Meaning and It Will Come
(Over Time)... 71
Devolution... 79
Pissing and Picking... 80
Reading Shit with a Sharp Edge 82
Fortune-Less Cookie 84
15:45:33 – 15:53:12 85
Doc... 87
My Shit-Stained Friend Who Exists On
Smoke Alone... 89
Quit Running and Embrace the Madness.................... 91

Blank Book Three (March)

Okay, We'll Be Friends Then 95
Decadence and Decay Every Day............................... 97
Between Every Fuck and Piss Time Passes 100
Lip and Lung Love of the Semi-Limbless Kind 105
A Dude and Some Drunk Bitch 107
Her and I 109
Sharing Spaces and Thinking.................................... 110
What am I Like?.. 115
Bukowski and Me (March 9, 1994) 116
12 Bucks and Almost a Free Pack of Cigarettes 119

I Hate It When 121
Superball 122
And I Feel That Time's A Wasted 124
Digesting Revenge 127
I Smile at Strange Things 128

Blank Book Four (March – April)

Moving Towards Some Plot 133
A Stream of Consciousness Writing 137
Bedroom Eyes Walks By 139
Bedroom Eyes' Lips 140
The Old Trout 141
I'm a Loser Baby So Why Don't You Kill Me 144
Trying to Find the Equilibrium 148
Fucking with the Drunk Poet Drunk and Sober 151
Hookers and Pimps 155
Eyeballs Are Like Chewing Gum 156
And I Sniff My Right Hand's Middle Finger 158
Corporate Takeover 159
The Old Trout (II) 160
Moving Through Whores 162
Our Skins Steamed Visibly 163
I'm a Little Bit Bitter 164
Invalid Theology 165
Tending Bar 166
Bedroom Eyes' Freckles 167
The Grift 169
You Know Who I'm Talking About 170
One Glorious Coffee with Sugar and Cream 172
The Old Trout (III) 173
Transactions 174
Stirred by a Passion 176

Blank Book Five (April – May)

Siren Trouble 183
My Paradigm Shifted 186
Kin 188
Purgative 189
Richard 191
Of All the Shit That Has Happened to Me 193
Royal Blue Scuffed Upon Navy Blue 197
Fucked-Up Love 199
I Got This Gift 200
Life Shuffles Across the Floorboards 202
No Sense of Direction 204
Chip Away 206
Something is Pinching 208
We 210
I've Had Enough 212
Dave (Fake Fucking Bastard) 214
A Song and Dance Routine 221
Collisional Gravity and a Court Date 225

Blank Book Six (May – August)

Just One Big Mouth, Please 231
Mike and Dike (A Poem in Two Acts) 233
I Should Have Been Hauled Away 240
Okay, This Is Getting Ridiculous 245
State of Mind 247
Salesmen and Flying 249
Pop! Pop! Down Goes the Enemy (My Generation) 254
The Heart Rises to the Throat 258
Shortly Before Death 260

Nature Will Catch Us While We're Sleeping
(if we're not careful) 262
Napkin Poem (Ladies Night) 263
Napkin Poem (Current State of Affairs) 265
Napkin Poem (Diary Entry of a Cigarette on the
Day It Dies) 266
Napkin Poem (Doggy Style on Texas-Hot Nights)...268
Dry Fucked Twice 269
Tripping in a Grocery Store 271
Dream #7093 (Spaghetti Head vs. the Ass Chairs)...273
White Trash Theater 274
Killing Voices 277
Some of the Best Words Were Never
Spoken At All 278
Distracted 279
One Big Scratch 281
I Am Not a Lush 282
The Young Are Restless 283
Forever Behind the Times 284
And If You Finally Catch Your Tail, Then What? 285
Where's the Finish Line? 286
Napkin Poem (Near Closing Time and During) 288
Waiting My Turn at Poetry Readings 290
Cauliflower Ears 292
Leaving Her 293
For Her 295
The Ballad of Skip (the gap-toothed one-eyed
lacklip without a nose) 296

Blank Book Seven (September – October)

Another Renaissance 301
Look Closer 304

Dim Getting Dimmer 305
Timeless Products 306
My Dead Self 308
Trying to Awaken the Muses.....................................309
Not For Sale 311
Where is the Fucking Passion? 314
Drunk Driving..316
The Absurdity and the Apocalypse 318
Red Capricorn 320
Free Dreaming I Naked of Everything Stop Sex 322
Prolegomenon (My Butt Sits Amongst the Rest)......324
Shut Your Fucking Mouth..329

Blank Book Eight (November – December)

Are You Going to Save Me? 333
Welcome to My Mind 335
Warfare with My Fears 338
Faces and Facades..341
Happy Birthday..344
Silence beneath the Bedpost 345
Good Fucks and Bad Fucks 347
Barroom Brawling 350
Punch Drunk and Without Bail 351
What Am I?..356
In a World of Shit...358

To Art
(the man and the pursuit)

"It started out as an exercise. I wrote of silences, of nights, I recorded the inexpressible. I fixed frenzies in their flight."

– Arthur Rimbaud, *A Season in Hell*, "Delirium II – Alchemy of the Word"

Introduction

I want to place Greg Gerding and his work in the context of Washington, D.C., 1994.

I had just moved to 16th and U Street. It was hip, it was now. The Anger Dad was dead, long live President Bill. Beer was cheap, the bookstores had vinyl. Long trippy kisses in the Zig Zag, walking on ice, Miles on the jukebox. Sundays, Domenick would let John host readings at his club. There on a jazz stage bigger than a postage stamp a shy bespectacled GQ gorgeous guy declared his virginity, "I'm nervous. This is my first time reading. This is a poem for my mom...." I started getting into it when he pissed on her head. Ah, a kindred spirit.

It's been a year since that night in Kala Kala. The readings are in Hell now. (Down 18th on the left.) Greg introduced many of these poems at that gathering. These are poems for the lips. These are poems for the hearth. They're personal, about fucking and drinking and being alone because we all fuck and drink and are alone. These poems are for you.

Eric Matchett
January 1995

Drunk. Blind love. No one cares. Being stupid. Saying stupid things. Drowning emotions really felt. Who cares? No one. Circles seen. Much like the motion of a flushing toilet. Real fun. No one cares about me. I just drink to forget. Yet I am sad. Why? No one cares. That's why. Continue drinking. Where to run? Nowhere. That's why you drink. Escape of the mind. Gone. No one cares. That really bugs me. Spinning. Just another shit down the toilet. Kimberly. Why? No one cares. Destruction of property. Much like the motion of a flushing toilet. I feel like putting my fist through a wall. Now anger. Alcohol oblivion. Forget them. I sip again.

BLANK BOOK ONE

January – February

Tabula Rasa

I was too young to understand as a child, but now I
know. The pain that I carried was not my own.

It was displaced pain put there by my mother.
Pain belonging to her lifetime of being abused.

I thought I was crazy.

But then I had an odd dream that brought me clarity.

In that dream, I was pissing on her head.
But the manner in which my piss dripped was artful.

Instead of it streaming down her face in torrents,
I could see that my piss became her tears.

And when I awoke, I understood the meaning.

I have never seen her cry
and I know that she needs to.

She is not the only one feeling the pain that she does.

Why does she bottle it up and lash out at those who
love her?

I throw my head back and pour alcohol into my skull
trying to erase the memories of my childhood.

Trying to get a clean start.

Bad Dream #1182
(Cats vs. Cars)

I am in my car
Sometimes passing
Sometimes being passed

Two cars blow past me and I can't take it anymore

I get off the highway and turn left down a side street

I slow down and find myself alone and it's getting dark

I look at the trees and the life that blooms around me

Just then, another fucking guy speeds past me on my left

I watch as the back of the asshole's car grows smaller and smaller

I see the back lights go bright briefly, then continue, then take a sharp right, and disappear

I continue along and come upon something writhing in the street

I stop my car and get out to investigate

It's a cat
It's just been struck by that asshole speeder

Its back is broken, and its front legs are crawling, while its back legs are dragging dead

I approach the cat, kneel down, and apologize
What else could I do?

I reach out, but it snaps at me in the only grotesque way that it can

I don't want it to bite or scratch me, but I don't want to leave it there to suffer either

So, I get back in my car and run over its head.

It was about then that I woke up,
horrified, confused, and sad.

Those Moments That Lie Just Beyond

Right after I was seated, I noticed there were a lot of gay men in the audience around me. I looked down at my program to avoid eye contact. I felt them staring.

During intermission, an older man approached my periphery.

He said to me, "My heart just jumped."

I thought, *Oh, no.*

But then I looked up and noticed he was the lead performer in this opera I was enjoying.

He continued, "Your profile is the splitting image of my son Bruno."

I tried to articulate my admiration for his ability, it was one of my first times to the opera.

He was clearly distracted and said, "Do you mind?"

And I said, "No."

He admired my profile one more time and then left.

The second half of his performance continued to stir me. How could such an old and small body frame emit such a powerful voice? It was like his body was a medium for something divine. His little old frame filled my head with such melody that I thought my head would explode.

The very ground seemed to thunder from his voice and I thought the whole building would crash down.

I saw him again afterwards and shook his hand.

I told him, "If I had been your son, I would have been a very proud son tonight."

To which his look replied that the sentiment was heartfelt.

"You are very kind for saying so."

Broadway-Bound Love

Pain and love.

I am running after you
yelling sentiments after you

and you are
just one step ahead of me

and all I can see is you
running ahead of me.

With outstretched hand,
I reach,

but only manage to touch
the satin which flows behind you.

I try to grasp
but cannot grab hold.

I continue to yell
let my poetry unfold.

And then
the pain

as you take a sharp left
and, as I gaze after your movement,
I slam face-first right into a wall
and fall on my back.

I watch everything spin,
and then go black.

You keep running.

Or do you?

Lewisburg Prison

Interviewer. Why are you here?

Prisoner. Why am I here? I killed! I killed my sister, her husband, her son, and the son's girlfriend. I also killed their dog just for the fuck of it. I slit all their throats and continued to stab them for the fuck of it.

Interviewer. Do you feel any remorse?

Prisoner. Well, I do forgive myself. I have learned to forgive myself and that's all that matters. People and society and The Man may not forgive me, but I forgive myself and that's all that counts. I forgive myself of my crimes and that's all that matters. I forgive myself. And so, here I sit.

Interviewer. What do you think about?

Prisoner. What do I think about? Escaping! What the fuck would you think about? I think about escaping this hell all the time. And then I realized that part of me escapes every day, so I think about that now.

Interviewer. Go on.

Prisoner. Like, well, hell. Okay, for example, I escape when I shit. When I take a shit, part of me makes it beyond these walls which surround me. Right? And I escape when I smoke. When I exhale smoke, I am exhaling a part of me that rises up and over these walls which surround me. Right? You see, what people and society and The Man don't know is that I am re-building myself on the other side of these walls. With my shit and my smoke, I am building a whole new me on the other side of these walls. It started with my feet and now it's up to my balls.

Interviewer. Please continue.

Prisoner. Shit and smoke are what I am becoming on the other side. In here, I am just a shell. While my true self is being built outside these walls. Meanwhile, I forgive myself. And shit and smoke as often as I can! *[laughs]* That way, I can finish growing and begin a new life on the outside. Outside these walls. Outside these fucking walls.

Imagining Suicide

Have you ever imagined what it would feel like
to take your own life?

Have you ever thought about
leaping ten stories
tipping your body over the edge
past the point of no return
flailing weightless
the sidewalk races up at you
and you feel your face hit the pavement?

Have you ever thought through
feeling the threads of a rope against your neck
as you balance yourself atop a chair
and then you kick the chair away
and feel your neck snap?

Have you ever thought through
putting a gun to your head
and feeling the cold steel of the gun
against your cheek?

Have you imagined pulling the trigger
and feeling hot lead shooting through your head?

But, what if you didn't do it right?
What if you are still alive?

You glance up at the bullet hole in the ceiling
and the bits of brain suspending from it.

You look down at the gun
and forget what you begun.

Instead, you are now hungry from stress
and a need to feed the loss in your head.

So you go to the kitchen to make some eggs,
but forget that eggs are supposed to be
prepared in a pan
and instead
you try cooking them
in your bare hand.

You start to wonder what smells funny
and question, "Why is it taking so long
for these eggs to scramble?"

as you run your hand back and forth over the flame.

Homeless Mail Veteran

I used to work behind a desk at a mall as a concierge and part of my job was selling postage stamps.

I remember a man who used to stand between traffic near that mall and approached cars and asked for change. He told me he was saving money so he could mail out some packages.

One day, he rolled up to my desk without his arms, without his legs, and without most of his torso. He spit out a bunch of change from his mouth that he had collected and asked me for a roll of stamps. I counted his coins and then tossed the roll of stamps into his mouth. He rolled away from my desk and left.

I later read a story about him in the newspaper. He had sent his legs to his parents, his arms to ex-employers, and his genitals to his ex-wife. The police found the remainder of him dead and propped up in an alleyway with stamps on his forehead and a mailing address tattooed across his chest. The newspaper would not divulge whose address it was, but the note that was found in his pocket indicated that the remainder of his torso and head were sacrificed as a political statement against all wars.

Five Cigarettes and a Pen
(Medium Point Bic Round Stic)

"Fuck you," I said, and then the candle went out.

I lit my cigarette with that candle
right before it went out.

Life unto life,
a vicious cycle.

I bent over, sucked life into my cigarette,
and sucked the life right out of the candle.

Too bad too,
it was a cool candle.
But my cigarette needed to be lit
in my drunken stupor.

Now, I can't even lift the lit cigarette to my lips.

A vicious cycle embodied
in a stupid game of life and death.

The death of a candle,
the life of a cigarette.

A life which is short-lived and short-died
and all comes around to…

"Fuck you," I said. And lit another cigarette.

Stamp one ash out and another sparks up.

"Fuck you," I said.

"Fuck you," I said.

Death and death and more death,
a vicious fucking cycle.

"Fuck you," I said.

And murdered another warm breath,
to feed my own slow death.

Guilt and the Senseless Stairmaster

I drank a whole pool of beer and smoked like a fool.
Now all I feel is gross and guilty.

I decide to punish myself further
by finally using that fitness membership
I have been paying for (and ignoring) for months now.

At the gym, there was a pool there too,
and a room full of fools
bobbing up and down on the Stairmasters.

Overcooked men and malnourished women
bobbing up and down for some reason
acting just as fake and getting next to nowhere,
like people at a bar lifting beers and mastering stairs to
relieve necessity.

Same scene,
different team.

A Cool and Peaceful Medium

Have you ever had one of those days when all the normal routines that help bring your being into a functional mode fail?

I had one of those days today.

I took my vitamins, but that just made my piss really colorful. I ate a decent breakfast, but that hardened into a brick in my stomach.

So, as soon as I got to work, I caved in and got myself a coffee, thinking that would be the cure.

I was excited too because I had purchased so many coffees that my next one was free. I, of course, picked out the most decadent one, the one with caramel and whipped cream and sprinkles and shit, and I was sure that would put a smile on my face and knock that terrible taste out of my mouth that accumulates from a night of excess. A night of drinking and smoking that had me waking up and going through the motions of preparing for work, except that the front of my brain was left somewhere on my pillow. I figured I'd function better without it, so I left it there to rest.

That horrible taste in my mouth led me to the only logical reason for its origin: I must have licked all my walls clean the night before. And, after licking all my walls, my tongue felt like I probably licked the cat clean too (except I don't have one).

And that damn free coffee didn't do the trick either. It mixed unpleasantly with the orange juice and toothpaste I had earlier trying to kill the taste of my walls and that cat.

And then I thought about the stew brewing in my stomach and couldn't stop thinking about the one direction I couldn't wait to send it in.

And then I sat at work.
And I sat at work.
And I sat at work.

And I was brewing and stewing and worrying that nothing would break me free of that state which was located somewhere far south of mediocrity.

And I began wishing for a happy medium.

And I began praying for a happy medium.

And then I caught myself praying and thought, *Fuck! This sucks. I never pray for anything.*

At that moment, I dropped everything and went outside for a walk.

And just stepping through that door was like an orgasm.

The sun gently stroked my face. I stopped thinking about smoking and licking walls and gross coffee. I only thought about the cool air and the snow on the ground. The snow-chilled sunshine breeze. It filled my lungs and filled my being, and I thought about being far away from work.

I then climbed the stairs to the top of the outdoor parking structure. Water dripped past my head. The snow-chilled sunshine breeze continued to fill my being. I climbed to the top and stepped out onto the snow-covered blacktop.

It was all very bright. And very, very beautiful. And very, very calm. And, in my mind, I thanked whoever put the barricades up against any cars reaching this top level. This cool, peaceful medium which I climbed up to and achieved and was right then admiring. An expanse of an inch of untainted snow. A virtual paradise far above all that nonsense.

I moved across the top of it. I was the first person who made any tracks through it. Only the sun was my witness and the wind whispered about my discovery to nobody listening. I continued to walk very slowly with my head down, because looking up and out at other buildings would have ruined that moment.

I imagined that the snow was transplanted from some place that was very far away. A block transported from somewhere pleasant left there for me to discover.

I started to think about love. Love as expansive and as untainted as that snow. And the space in my head, which I had left on my pillow, started to fill with thoughts of love.

My being continued to be filled with the snow-chilled sunshine breeze and I started feeling really good. I waved as I moved quickly north past mediocrity and was empowered by new discovery, beauty, and love.

I thought about being alone and I was not afraid. I felt as though I could carry myself across an eternity of that, and never be bored, and never grow old.

My being became a bottle of good feelings.

I reluctantly returned to work, but continued thinking about snowy expanses, sunshine, beauty, and love. I clung to those thoughts to maintain a cool and peaceful medium.

A Couple of Hours Later

With love on my mind and a cool breeze in my heart, I had to get away from work again and try to recapture the moment of a few hours ago.

It was still empowering, but in a more worldly kind of way.

The breeze was now a cold wind, but the sun continued to blind. To my dismay, on top of the parking structure, a single pair of tire tracks now circled the snowy expanse, exposing the blacktop beneath.

My earlier discovery had since been violated.

I moved down the right side of the structure all the way to the end and looked out at a bustling highway, pulsing, like cells through a vein.

I circled around and walked down the other side and tried to create the same feeling I had hours before. But the tire tracks interrupted my meandering.

I looked over at the footsteps I just made and thought, *No matter how hard I look for my tracks in the future, I continue to be distracted by the clearly visible tracks of my past.*

And I try to make a return.

And I cry about a return.

But, it's no use.

I must tread on,
blinded by the sun.

And I must move on,
on into my future.

A Couple More Hours Later

I finally get off work and make one more trip to the top of the parking structure. I look at what has now become familiar and is no longer new.

The love on my mind still lingers.

The cool breeze now simply makes my ears cold.

The footsteps of my past are still visible, but are now slightly less discernible.

It is my dream that these footsteps of my past are packed solid, so that once the blacktop is exposed, my snow-packed footsteps will still remain.

The cells continue to pulse.

I light a cigarette and think about the shot of vodka I will be drinking later.

And I wish, I don't pray, I wish that the words will continue to roll.

And I hope that my footsteps will always have soul.

A Wise Man Moved Slowly Past My Bench One Day

I am sitting on a bench in the middle of the day. There's snow melting in the sun and it's pulsing water onto the pathway.

I'm thinking about a love I just recently lost. I lost her because when I thought about love, it was not her face that I imagined. So, she left.

So, I sit here and wonder what my fucking problem is.

I look at the ice-covered tennis court, and the ice-covered basketball court, and I follow the path of the occasional passerby, and I watch as they slowly move through or around a large accumulation of water at the bottom of a slope in the pathway.

And I look at my hands. And I kick with my feet. And I think. And I look. And I look. And I think.

Then, an old man comes slowly along the pathway and I watch him.

He says, "Hello."

I say, "Hey."

He then continues on his way. But, before he gets to the large puddle, he slows to a stop. He stoops down very slowly and he rolls up his pant legs and then he moves very slowly through the large puddle.

And I watch him. And I think, *Now there goes a wise man who has been down this path before. I wonder if he could solve my problems regarding love?*

But then I think that I just witnessed the only lesson he has to give. He, having been down this path before, took his knowledge of his past and avoided soiling his pant legs (again).

And I think that even if I were to stop him and ask him about love, he would probably say, "Roll up your pant legs before you go strolling on in."

Have You Ever Seen Anything As Silly?

Have you ever seen anything as silly as speed walkers rushing by, in a mall, past fast-food restaurants?

They look so silly.

So much motion,
such
slow
motion.

Doing so much,
to
do
so
little.

With great determination.

And
getting

nowhere

fast.

Spaghetti before Sex

Sitting before a blank page, I am taking inventory of everything around me which makes everything all right. The words are not coming, but everything still seems all right.

There's plenty of beer in the fridge and a vodka back-up in the freezer.

There's a new pack of cigarettes.

There are four lit candles.

There's Tchaikovsky spinning on the record player.

And there's buttercream legs wrapped within black stockings (that go all the way up) preparing a fine meal of spaghetti.

But then the record stops, and the flame spits at me, demanding me to bring forth some words. And then the fitness-freak neighbor begins marching on her ski machine on the hardwood floors above. She sounds like an army on my head.

However, with the smell of tomato and garlic, and the promise of love, I have much to look forward to.

Because no matter how much the flame spits and the army marches above, I just cannot squeeze poems from my pen, or force a rape upon paper.

Creatures of the World, Unite!
(Hit Those Little Motherfuckers)

Do you speed along in your car because you are young? Do you enjoy pushing 90 on the highway and through back roads because you think you will never get caught?

No, you speed along because you have yet to fuck up the equation; that sum of small animals you've struck with your car, because you drove too fast or developed poor reaction skills. You reach critical mass at around one deer, three squirrels, two birds, one cat, and a dog named "Puff" (who you thought probably deserved a roadside death anyway).

It is that equation which adds up to you minding your speed on the highway and on back roads. You fuck up enough little lives and you start to slow down. It isn't age, it isn't the dust of youth, it isn't the volume of tickets which deplete your meager existence, it is this sum total of death which begins to take its toll on your car and your life.

You start to think about "Puff" and the small boy to whom he brought joy; a joy crushed for a few saved seconds, a few saved seconds trying to make it to your stupid TV program in time.

Meanwhile, little did you know, little death was just for show. Little squirrels, little birds, little cats, little dogs, they all know what you don't know. They were at the last rally. They attended the last meeting. They are little, but they are little calculating bastards.

Each little death is a little planned suicide. Each little death is accounted for and mourned among the little souls and each little newborn. Don't be fooled. Don't think you move slow because you are old. Don't let those little motherfuckers even gain an inch, because they know that with each slowed car, it's a minor triumph, a successful suicide which has affected another motorist and helped them reach their ultimate goal.

A group of birds on the side of the road, don't be fooled, is just a small protest, a tiny demonstration in the ongoing battle to take back what was once theirs. These little birds are causing the stir. They know that they are too small to cause a blemish, so they continue to whisper their rhetoric into the cow and the moose, and when that works, all hell will break loose.

Their goal? To turn all signposts back into trees, and all highways and back roads back into streams. But don't be fooled by this small, silent social movement that exists among the little creatures and the ignorant larger creatures because it isn't your age that is making you slow, it is the little ones that are chipping at your soul and attempting to take back the show.

Poor Little Jimmy

Self-described martyr,
self-described bohemian,
self-described artist and writer.

Poor little Jimmy,
not a key on his ring
and barely a pea for a brain.

Anger is his passion,
and sex is on his mind,
he would sell his stuff for a dime
or a lime.

He thinks he understands
and would eat shit from my hand,
if he wasn't a self-described Jesus.

The only room he can claim as his own
can be located in the upper left-hand corner of his head.

It is there where he makes his bed
and he imagines sharing the same head
with Kurt Vonnegut.

I imagine Jimmy inside his own head,
on top of his bed,
while on the other side of his skull
he yells across the way to Kurt
who is sitting there with his knees to his chest
and is dreading sharing the same space with
poor little Jimmy.

Poor little Jimmy
thinks that his self-described anger
expressed through his art
is more poetic than the fact that he
hasn't got a key on his ring.

If he wrote about the realities of his existence
that might be more valuable than his angry insistence
and come across with much more sincerity.

I have a difficult time with a self-described *anything*
who comes up to my face and tells me that he
is a bohemian artist.

It is people who label others,
you should not label yourself
and tout that which is not really there.

If he is looking for money and fame,
then he should write about his keyless chain
and the pea named "Kurt" in his brain.

Bored with Myself

You want food for thought?

Imagine that every time you played a record
you shoved the needle into the artist's vein
and tapped right into their brain
and you saw the pain
and you saw the insane
and you saw the rain on the windowpane
and you saw the train move through a white plain
and you saw everything that the artist saw when they
were inspired –

could you take it?

Petty Fears and Philosophies Expressed at a Bare Bar Between a Middle Easterner and an American Who Just Won't Go Very Far

American. In America – you work – and then, you die. That's it.

Middle Easterner. Okay.

American. If the taxpayers don't get ya – then the FBI will. The FBI will crack your fuckin' shoulder blade! I'm not trying to scare you, I'm just telling you how it is in America.

Middle Easterner. I had a wife – I had a kid – and – I had a girlfriend.

American. I don't have a wife – I don't have a kid – because my Dad is dying. Well anyway, what happened to your wife?

Middle Easterner. She wanted to work.

American. What?! What's wrong with that?

Middle Easterner. I tell her, "You are the wife, you stay at home." So, she left.

American. Well, I think women should be self-supportive.

Middle Easterner. That is my girlfriend, NOT my wife.

American. You must be some kind of sex machine.

Middle Easterner. Well, she fuck me up the ass, so I fuck her up the ass!

(Their gaze shifts to the news on the television)

Middle Easterner. That is a Libyan terrorist.

American. No, that's an FBI agent about to crack somebody's ass.

Planning For Your Birth

1.
With this blank book, I started from the beginning and couldn't wait until the end. So, I flipped the book around and started a beginning from the end.

Now, I can't wait to put it all together and figure out the middle. The ending to the middle is a much easier process than the beginning to the end.

2.
Imagine for a minute, if you started with your death, instead of your birth.

You pull your dead body up out of your own grave and begin life at age 80 and start working towards your youth. Instead of planning for your funeral, you start planning for your birth.

You find a nice, willing woman and you negotiate rent for her womb. Then you settle your estate and move in sometime during age day one. And with the same old hands that lifted you from death, you take those now infant hands and spread those legs to enter into birth.

With the rent paid for the next nine months, you begin a slow shrinking into nothingness.

Common Sense

It amazes me sometimes how the most basic processes of life and common sense manage to evade so many people. Daily. Hourly.

I live with one now who lacks common sense in finances, or just answering the telephone.

You would think that the basic lesson in finance is that you don't spend money that you don't have. If it isn't in the bank, or under your account, or in your hot little hand, then, DON'T spend it.

If the telephone rings and you are in the shower with shampoo in your hair, what do you do? Do you do what she did? Hop out of the shower, run wet through the apartment, and while turning the corner in her nakedness, slip on the floor, slam into the door, slink down on all fours, and miss the telephone anyway?

And sitting there with a banged knee and a bleeding toe, do you wonder why you did so? Especially when you have an answering machine AND a cordless telephone.

This is some advice from me to you: quickly buy some common sense with some credit you can't afford and phone information for a clue because they'll understand.

BLANK BOOK TWO

February – March

Frogs in Tysons Corner, Virginia

"What do you mean 'Peace Frogs?'" this old bitch asks me, who looks like she has had an easy life. A life protected by the innocence of the WORD and the ignorance of the FAITH.

"What do you mean, what do I mean?"

"I mean, what does the 'Peace Frogs' thing mean?"

And I attempt to explain it to her, but it's like talking to someone who is high on heroin.

She only approached me so that she could do her little favor for God. She looks at me like I am a lost sheep who needs to be collected and taught.

She says, "Well, did you know that, in the Bible, God sent down a plague in the form of frogs to kill all the sinners?"

"Yes, someone told me this last week."

"Well, so, how can they be 'Peace Frogs?' I would never want a frog on me, on my body, in my bed, or anywhere near me for that matter. How can they be 'Peace Frogs!?!'"

"The frog is an old Shaman icon for peace..." I explain, but it's no use. She is already getting out her little literature which will make me understand, which will convert me to Christianity, and which will suddenly make me despise frogs and, subsequently, quit my job. And my new job will be wandering through malls, looking for lost sheep to collect. She hands me her little literature and I accept it because I am so fucking considerate.

She asks again, "Why 'Peace Frogs?'"

I try a different tack, "Okay, so, seriously, just like in the Bible this product is like that plague. It is expanding and suckering all the sinners into buying Peace Frogs T-shirts and shorts so that when Christ comes down again, his job of eliminating all the sinners will be that much easier. All he will have to do is find everybody with a 'Peace Frog' on their person and smite them. In a way, we are doing God's work also. We are making his job easier by distributing the symbol of sin and plague and death. Pretty soon, we will be everywhere. And everyone who has ever sinned will wear our clothes and you will know to avoid them because they are the soon-to-be smote."

And then, as if I said nothing, she adds, "Even when I was little I stayed away from frogs because I thought they were slimy and I didn't want to touch them."

"So, even before reading the Bible and understanding the frog, you knew? You knew, even then, when you were really little that the frog was evil?"

"Oh yes," she says, "even then, I knew." She then insists, "Read that pamphlet. And let me tell you, I will never buy one of those 'Peace Frogs.'"

"Oh really, you feel so free from sin?"

"Oh yes, I love God wholeheartedly." And she walks away.

I read her literature and the little, little fine print and it says:

1. You must recognize that you are a sinner. Why? Because the Bible says so.

2. You must love God and Jesus with all your heart. Why? Because the Bible says so.

And I think, *Well, this is all fine and dandy, but what does the Bible say about finding a new apartment when you have nowhere to go and no money to do so?*

As I see it, I have two options:

1. Keep my sinful job and continue to sell the plague and reap small rewards. Small rewards like a place to sleep and food to eat (and hopefully a beer and a cigarette a week).

2. Embrace the WORD and accept the FAITH and wander homeless and aimless through a mall protected by a God who doesn't house or feed me.

I think I will choose the former, because I don't much like sleeping outside in the cold and my stomach is tired of digesting itself over and over and over again.

Grill Me a Slice of Change and Hold the Onions

My life is changing. And change is strange.

It is strange how the feeling of finally hitting a baseball over the centerfield fence is now akin to the same feeling as marveling at my own contribution to the ever-growing collection of empty vodka bottles and empty beer cans and spent cigarette butts in my apartment. It is starting to resemble a landscape I would feel proud connecting a Lionel train set through.

Change is strange.

How Budweiser begot Light, and then the two became Dry. And how, in my mind, this equation suddenly becomes all-encompassing in illustrating the lifecycle of a relationship. I've even used it in actual conversation, as if revealing some deeper truth.

"Don't you see? Budweiser begot Light, and then the two became Dry. See?"

And how, when I order a sandwich without onions at the fast-food joint, it suddenly becomes an abbreviation sent to God.

"I would like to order the Grand Ham sandwich with mustard and no onions."

It is repeated through a microphone from the order taker to the maker, so loud that I can hear the amplification of his voice in the kitchen behind him.

"One Grand H, with an M, and an L, and a T, but hold the O."

And "hold the O" echoes through my mind until it produces a thought which I didn't think it could produce sober, which was, *And if you hold that "O" really straight, I might be able to nail it with my erection.*

And then I think about my limp dick.

And then I feel concern for my limp dick which does not like this whole change thing and has obviously made this fact known by displaying inactivity. Not even a stirring.

And then I become depressed about my strange change.

And I think about how bland my sandwich tastes without "O."

And then I shrug and think, *Well, you asked for it, you eat it.*

I Am Not Complaining

But why is it that the ones who feel the most comfortable approaching me are the really weird ones?

I am not complaining because I love that a girl, who is still in high school, can come up to me and talk to me about nothing while smoking a cigarette and then suddenly show me her breasts through a thin white T-shirt and share with me the fact that she just recently got, not just one nipple, but both nipples pierced and I look as strange shapes protrude through her T-shirt and I am aroused by this.

There is something sexy about someone who wants, and gets, their various body parts pierced by sharp metallic objects and now proudly displays these piercings like one might proudly display a picture of their child. Well, close to that. Maybe more like how one might display a desire or a fear like a badge on their chest. Or did I just answer my own question?

Anyway, they are not weird ones, they just suddenly become brave through the extreme, having not one nipple, but both nipples pierced, suddenly empowers them with balls the size of a Texas mentality to approach that which they most desire. And they most desire me.

Or do I just flatter myself?

Whatever the case may be, those other women who only pass a flirtatious glance in my direction, the ones who make eye contact, soften their eyes, and, maybe subconsciously, slightly part their lips at me, an action that is ever so little, but does not go unnoticed. This is a message to you. You do not have to resort to the extreme just to gain enough confidence to approach me, the object of your desire.

Or do I just flatter myself?

Meanwhile, I will rejoice in those with pierced body parts and pierced eggs from sperms of promised love that continue to approach me, and through their extremities and their tragedies possess enough confidence to come up to me and at least tell me their name. Because flattery and attention does give me an erection and that sucks because it is so rare that anybody approaches me.

Do I look like the type who bites? Do I possess the face of someone who causes pain and hurt?

Because if I do, continue to stay away, and allow the extremities and the tragedies to approach me and flatter me and suck me and fuck me, because people with pierced body parts seem to indicate to me a sign of maturity.

So, to all those ones with flirtatious glances, keep on running by with trimmed split ends and your pussy in your hands and your eyes in your head, because I would much rather prefer one who depends on a pierced body part to keep their level of sanity and attain a level of confidence that allows them to speak their mind.

Daydream #133,880
(I Often Picture Women Naked)

I hold you close and kiss your rich, full lips.

I work my hands all over your body, passing them over your tight ass in jeans and then up across your back and down again. I slide one hand up to your hair where I stroke it and then gently grab hold. I pull your head back and suck at your neck.

I outline your breast with my other hand and move it down over your flat stomach and, ever so lightly, I press on your pussy through your clothes and then move my hand back up to your perfect breast.

I unbutton your top and admire your chest in that barely capable bra, your breasts are bulging beautifully around the edges. I lower your bra straps down around your shoulders until your nipples are exposed. I kiss and tongue your gorgeous breasts and tease your nipples until they are erect.

I then work my way down to your bellybutton and place my tongue inside that space and I can tell you like this by the way your body's squirming. While kissing and tonguing your mid-section, I unbutton your jeans and pull them down and off. No underwear, that's nice.

I then work my tongue towards your pussy. I pause there for a moment to admire your beautiful youth and the immaculate folds you possess down below. I spread your lips slightly with my fingers and, with my tongue and my mouth, I make love to your pussy.

It is at this moment that you know.

You know the universe, and the distance of the stars, and my tongue upon your clit.

Then, all you can think about is my cock splitting you wide and filling that ache that is mounting in your youthful little pussy.

And I give it to you.

And you don't know what to do. You've already had two orgasms from my tongue and now you possess my cock and you don't know what to do.

Your pussy becomes so wet that you start thinking about the purity of rain and the volume of a storm as it rushes to your groin and envelops my cock and gushes forth.

And you scream into blissful heavens.

And your pussy feels so good that you unknowingly shred my back with your fingernails.

And you want to touch your pussy but you know that it can't feel any better than it does right now.

With my cock inside, and the rain pouring down.
Pounding and screaming.

A Six-Pack and Who Gives a Flying Fuck

Sitting before blank pages that I know need to be filled and I know will eventually be filled, I let my pen fly aimless, while I sit, a passive observer, a slave to the absurdity of my flying moving hand as words spread on the page like water through a paper towel.

Spreading, spreading, spreading,
and filling, filling, filling....

Only to be squeezed for meaning that may not be there.

Squeezing a wet paper towel and hoping for one last beer that will help maintain the stupor that continues to keep the hand moving and flying across the page.

Squeezing and squeezing and squeezing....

Until there is nothing left but a puddle of piss and these words filling page after page, aimless and drunk. With a little beer left, and much less hope for meaning.

There is no beer left.
Good night.

My Refuge Up Above It All

I return to the top floor of the empty parking structure and what was once a paradise just a week ago. All the snow is gone and there is just a puddle rippling towards death, running from the sun.

This is a return to the reality, a relief from the monotony, and a cleansing of my mind.

I take it all in and I gulp in clean air and then I sigh and move to wherever my feet take me. I move against the stiff wind and I imagine that it is not the wind but my motion struggling against the proper rotation of the earth. I am trying to maintain my balance as I continue to head in clearly wrong directions.

I close my eyes and fight on anyway.

There is a brief calm from the wind. I open my eyes and see printed on the cold, stone pavement before me the word "EXIT" painted there with an arrow pointing straight ahead.

I think to myself, *If only things were that easy.*

I move in that direction until I come to another "EXIT" and an arrow pointing to the left. But instead of going left, I continue going straight ahead. Fuck what it says to do.

I move close to the end of the parking structure, but not right up to the edge of it, because just a four-floor drop does not agree with my petty, annoying fear. Not a fear of death, death would be an easy flight off this parking structure, but rather a fear of a continuous freefall. Like, if I fell, I would never stop, I would just flail forever through space anticipating a bone-crushing splat that never comes.

I stop at another "EXIT" in the pavement with an arrow pointing in the direction I just came from and I think of how foolish all the poets are who ever try to write that "immortal poem," because whoever first painted the word "EXIT" upon the cold, concrete ground with an arrow indicating the correct direction is the greatest poet who ever lived.

And you can see his work everywhere.

You Have Got to Have a Sense of Humor

Sometimes I laugh at tragedy and awful things because I have to make light of all the absurdity and senselessness that comes with daily living. It's my survival mechanism.

Someone just told me about a man who could have died if the golf ball that skipped off his head had nailed him square instead. She described how the ball skipped off his head and how later no hair would grow there.

I laughed so hard when I heard this.

Imagine a man out there with a streak on his head from some freak golfing incident. Why don't we read about these kinds of stories in the newspaper? I would find the newspaper much more interesting then.

This same man not only had a bald streak atop his head from an errant golf ball, but he also lopped off his own toe while mowing his lawn. He ran over his own foot and cut off his toe. He picked it up, showed it to his wife, and she screamed. She then drove him to the hospital while he held his toe in his hand. He was in a state of shock, but they managed to reattach it.

I laughed so hard when I heard this too.

Isn't it funny how you can laugh at serious trauma in retrospect? I nearly lost my nose to a dog, but I still love dogs. I was smacked in the face with a baseball the first time my dad took me out to play catch, and I still play baseball. I almost plucked out my eye with a #2 pencil, but I still like writing.

Because if you don't laugh, you'll cry.

I feel a certain kinship to this man who faced similar traumas to mine and probably found himself teeing off the following weekend and mowing his lawn the following month, he probably approached both with just a little more caution and was a little more aware.

You have to laugh, because if you don't you will likely die from a stressed-out heart and a too-careful eye. Plus, there's nothing fun about being so serious about everything anyway.

Squeeze It for Meaning and It Will Come (Over Time)

I don't even know where to start.

I sit here and try to put everything together in my mind, everything that has been blown apart within the past week. I will start with that which immediately surrounds me.

A vodka bottle, new and all but full, after two shots done and thinking about a third. A first, a second, and soon a third, to be shot from a glass with a horse-drawn carriage printed on its side with gothic-print "Amish Country" written across it on a glass made in Taiwan.

A single beer waits to be cracked. I think about how it is becoming easier for me to shrug off shots and now I consume less beer, which is cool because money is virtually non-existent, but paper and ink are plenty.

So, here I sit having finished my third and thinking of a fourth and seeing how long I can hold out before cracking my one and only beer.

My one and only beer. Somehow, that fact needed repeating since I most recently left a situation in which beer in the fridge was abundant and literally seemed to fuck itself into larger populations on its own. My new fridge is unpracticed and old with an infertile penis, and perhaps I will make some sense of this writing sometime tomorrow, sober.

Meanwhile, I will try to coach my new fridge into fertility and a more active sex life, because buying whores just isn't going to do it. The fridge is going to have to find some inner peace within itself and start producing me some fucking beer!

So, here I sit having thrown back my fourth and my one and only beer remains unopened. And I think about saying, *Fuck my beer*, and returning it to the unproductive, dry, old fridge and then returning my old sorry lame old ass back to my dry, unproductive lame old page and continuing to suck shots from the bottle because I no longer wince, nor even frown.

Is it "nor" or "or?"
Or is it "or" or "nor?"
I think it's "nor" not "or."
But I could be wrong. It could be "or" and not "nor."

Oh, who gives a fuck?

And now I discard the silly Amish glass made in Taiwan and wrap my big silly lips around the bottle and suck and suck and suck like a baby at a breast. And I relax like a baby at a breast. And I wish I were like a baby and were sucking on some breasts.

But, I feel a special camaraderie with the unproductive and dry old fridge, while I listen to Jim Morrison sing his stupid shit and begin to feel sick, not from the bottle, but from a thought that Jim Morrison never knew who the fuck he was or what the fuck he did.

And then I think about the 60s. And then I think about social movements. And then I think about bullshit. And then I return to this past week.

And then I return to that beautiful vodka breast and I suck and I suck and I suck, without a wince. And I feel proud and I feel glad that, because I have no money, my stomach will digest itself to a smaller size and it will require less food and, therefore, I will require less alcohol to get more fucked up.

And I will finally achieve the look I have always aspired for: pale and emaciated like death, skinny and cheekless like a drug addict. And that brings a smile to my lips somehow. Because a look and feel of death appeals to me.

And Morrison woke up this morning and got himself a beer. And he let it roll, baby, roll all night long. And I let my pen roll, baby, roll all night long. And I am now numb to the realities of this past week.

And I smile at an aspiration for death. And perspiration resulting in death. And a respiration killed just for the sake of death. And I know I will find meaning in this tomorrow.

And I wrap my lips. And I wrap my lips. And I wrap my lips. Fuck it. I lose count.

Just imagine my mouth around the nipple sucking and hoping for erection. Yes, find the meaning. Find the meaning before I spray it all over your face and spread it all over your cheeks.

And now I try to move back from the immediate and I become sick with thoughts of work on a Saturday in Retail Hell in the middle of a mall where just removing a shoe to scratch at my foot makes me feel like I am exposing my genitalia and am scratching at my balls.

And where rubbing my nose makes me so self-conscious that my biggest fear then becomes that all my rubbing did is knock a booger loose and now it is hanging there and with each breath in and out, that booger is doing chin-ups with my nose and everybody is too disgusted, or too distracted, to say anything.

And so they don't. And there I am scratching at my genitalia with boogers doing chin-ups from my nose AND I'm having a bad hair day.

And now Morrison is reduced to Muzak on the mall sound system. And I think, *That lucky bastard, in life and in death.*

And then I become so stressed with all the activity of shit from this past week that the bald man with the hairy back and the crooked yellow teeth working next to me freaks me out. Or maybe he freaks me into a state of numbness and speechlessness.

And the balding man with Vaseline hair strands who works on my other side suddenly frightens me with his bad jokes and the enthusiasm with which he laughs at them, and I begin to freak out. Or maybe freak into a state similar to the one of my new fridge: in need of beer and the need of a female's breasts pressed up against me and presented to my wide open mouth.

And how my greatest fear now suddenly becomes a fear of balding and being capable of storing a wealth of bad jokes within a head of bad teeth.

Please continue squeezing until that meaning comes.

I take another drag off the bottle and begin recalling my night, the night before, and how I sucked down eight beers with my new roommate and spent money I pretended to have, or I actually had and no longer have.

And I think, *I bet that motherfucker Jim Morrison never realized how many free beers he consumed. How many free bottles he consumed. How many young breasts he consumed and...*

He and his snake, which is seven miles long, ride his snake, he's old and his skin is cold.

"The west is the best."

Way to change the subject you unknowing and unrealizing motherfucker.

With all those beers and all those bottles and all those breasts you never even realized you sucked. You suck!

Meanwhile, I recall everything from the night before. Sucking down eight beers and sucking down a free coffee at a local coffeehouse. Oh sure, coffee is free, keep me awake and aware. But no, my beer couldn't be free so I could sleep and be asleep and dream instead of weep.

And *"This is the end/ Beautiful friend/ This is the end/*

My only friend, the end/ It hurts to set you free/ But you'll never follow me/ The end of laughter and soft lies/ The end of nights we tried to die/ This is the end."

Fuck you, motherfucker! You never knew the end.

The end is when you are lying in bed in cold/hot sweats trying to decide whether it is more comfortable to lie in sweat with a blanket on or lie in sweat ice with the blanket off....

(Interlude: I have finished with the breast and have finally cracked my one and only beer.)

...Cold/hot sweats in bed, and you lie there in bed, you don't sleep, you lie there, holding in your gas because you are afraid of what might go shooting out of your ass. And you tell your quickly beating heart to hang in there and keep up with the inert marathon, and keep up with the rapid motion of the off and on blanket. And you pause to remind yourself to breathe. And then you worry because now breathing has become an effort. And, *this* is the end, beautiful friend. When breathing becomes a mental process. And your ass doesn't know whether to fart or shit. And your body doesn't know whether to melt or freeze. This is the end, you motherfucker. This is the end that you were unaware of.

And now I listen to Perry Farrell. And here is another motherfucker who doesn't know what he had. But, he had a dad, big and strong, and when he turned around, he found his daddy gone. His daddy has gone away.

Farrell used to grunt real well and now he merely sighs.

And he should consider numbness and death and hope that his dad becomes reduced to Muzak in a mall.

And this is going nowhere, as I sip on my beer. But keep squeezing and maybe, just maybe, the meaning will come. Or maybe not, who gives a fuck?

Well, I would like to say some really hateful shit against my ex-girlfriend now, whose fridge produces beer babies. But I have suddenly become numb, but am unfortunately still aware that I breathe and exist.

And Farrell screams, *"Sex is violent!"*

And I think, *Tell me about it. That's what I miss! But not for much longer....*

And maybe that is the most hateful thing that could fall upon my ex-girlfriend's ears. That I am laying my erection into better pussy. And, yes, I can write "pussy" because it is much easier than writing "vagina."

And now my words, like my pen, are ink. They're ink lying on this page like I would like to be lying in bed, asleep. Like these words suddenly laid upon the page, asleep. Words: ink laid asleep on the page, to be awakened by a mind, or an eye, or an imagination, or a voice. And...

"I was standing in the shower thinking/ About what makes a man"

"Water hits my neck/ And I'm pissing on myself"

And I miss the Farrell of old. And I miss the fridge of youth which produces beer babies. But I don't miss the pussy that comes with it. Because I erect for bigger and better things. And maybe that is the most hateful thing I can write against my ex. Bigger and better breasts. Bigger and better pussy. Bigger and better human being. You god-damned fucking bitch!

With your petty fears of loneliness and reality and responsibility and life. A life filled with cold/hot sweats and shit shooting out your ass.

And now I just want to concentrate on Farrell, and on what Jane says, and imagine the ocean breaking on the shore and coming together with no harm done and sipping on my one and only beer and moving on.

Devolution

I didn't just crash,
I simply passed out.

And I didn't thank God,
I thanked the bed for breaking my fall.

Pissing and Picking

I'm thinking about the old man I saw earlier today.

He was hunched over the sink in the public restroom and was picking the bits of lunch from between the teeth he just removed from his skull.

He finished and backed away.

Soon after that, I shook the piss from my dick and returned it to my pants and backed away. I watched him return the teeth back to his skull.

He moved over to the urinal I forgot to flush and I moved over to the sink and looked at the old man's lunch, stuck to the bottom of the sink.

I thought about puking, but I washed my hands anyway, consciously aware of the fact that the old man's lunch was so close to my hands. So close, that I could feel the heat on the backs of my hands that those morsels were emitting.

We continued maneuvering around each other in the small confines of that bathroom.

I would not enjoy trading shoes with this old man, not even for a day. I want my teeth to remain right where they are, as I check them for food in the mirror, still one with my mouth.

The day I start trading in real body parts for plastic ones is the day I cash in my chips and call it a day. A long, hard day.

Reading Shit with a Sharp Edge

It is strange being recognized in a small place in Adams Morgan and receiving praise for the shit which I read while drunk, for the shit which was recently written drunk.

I take it in as people talk to me and surround me and ask questions and offer advice, and I just sit there grinning and drunk.

People go up and dedicate their shit to me and read their shit sober, their shit which was obviously, painstakingly written sober. I am jealous.

And they thank me?
I nod, drunk.

I wish somebody would buy me a beer, but they don't. They just talk to me and talk to me, surrounding me with words.

Don't get me wrong, they are words I appreciate, but they are words I don't feel worthy of being surrounded with because I write drunk, and I think they know I write drunk, because I write stuff about being drunk.

I make my way home by breaking through their words and surrounding myself with my car.

I get home.
Nobody's home.

I pull out my book and some unidentifiable shit is stuck on it. I decide to remove it with the same razor I shave my face with.

I cut into the book and remove the shit by removing some of the covering with my sharp razor blade. I imagine that it must be the same kind of sharp intellect that must cut into my covering to get past all my shit.

I yearn for something I can feel proud of because it was written painstakingly and written during a fit of sobriety and something which I feel I invested a lot of time in, sober.

Instead, I find myself shaving my book,
in the bathroom,
alone.

Wondering why, and wondering
about a lot of things.

Fortune-Less Cookie

Why was it that I put so much hope into that fortune cookie I was about to crack open?

I was reduced to giddy anticipation, like it was going to reveal some kind of spark or inspiration, like some positive change was going to be presented to me from the middle of that fucking fortune cookie.

And like divine intervention, a fist of divine will came crashing from above and what was revealed to me from within that fortune cookie was… nothing.

Nothing!

Not one god-damned fucking thing. Not even a receipt to at least tell me that, yes indeed, I did just eat, and that, yes indeed, I am validated and do exist, and that, yes indeed, I did just crack open that fucking fortune cookie in giddy anticipation of something.

But no, nothing.

I asked for another after deciding I would tempt fate one more time. Cruel, ironic bitch that she is.

15:45:33 – 15:53:12

(15:45 and 33 seconds.)

I am sitting in my chair, bored. I'm staring at the cash register which digitally flashes military time and has this crappy little feature that torturously ticks off each and every second of each and every day.

There is no business and nothing left to do but think that the sandwich I just ate for lunch did not agree with me. I feel like I ate a small dog. Fur and all. Fur and alive. Just held that small dog's head in one fist while the other clutched its rear end and I took a large bite right into its side. Through hair, through skin, through meat. And then, like I was some savage wild beast, I just sat there and chewed while that small dog bled on my lap. That's what feels like is sitting in my stomach right now: a small, hairy, gross dog.

Then, the strange man who tends after all the plants walks right up to me, as he does often now, and asks me if I am bored yet, and I reply that I have been bored for quite some time.

He says, "Well, I was just in the storage room reading and taking a nap."

I say, "I am so jealous."

He says, "Why? Can't you take a nap here?"

I survey my kiosk sitting naked in the middle of the mall, laugh, and say, "No."

He says, "That's too bad, I have been taking naps for the past four weeks."

Then he shuffles away with his bucket in his hand.

And I am filled with jealousy. And also filled with a small, hairy, gross dog that is now barking in my stomach. And I am trapped here in military time, filling each goose-step with wishes that I never had to eat, or sit here, or think…

think, think…

think, think…

(15:53 and 12 seconds.)

Doc

I just spoke to a man whose nickname is "Doc."

"Doc" has been around for awhile and drunk a lot of beer and smoked a lot of cigarettes and claims that he can tie a knot in a cigarette, even though I have never seen him do it.

I just met him.

Doc looks like he has seen a lot of shit, so I ask him if he has ever been out in the cold, imagining that he might have some kind of hard-luck story about being homeless in Alaska.

He says, "Hell yeah! I work in the frozen food section of that grocery store in Falls Church."

And I think, *Wow. That's disappointing.*

Then he tells me about the time he was in a full body cast and was selling newspapers on a corner in 90-degree weather, just so he could help support his mom. That was kind of impressive.

He vows that he will get married when he turns 41. I have a hard time believing him, but I respect him and his desires just the same.

Doc was stopped for a DUI back in 1983 and spent three days in jail because his blood/alcohol level was 3.1, and then he later blew a 3.5, and he was going for a 4.0, which would have been a perfect drunk.

Without a motorcycle license and without a job, he landed himself in a jail cell at his mother's house and this job at the grocery store in Falls Church in the frozen food section freezing his ass off and not caring because he anticipates a wife at 41.

He withstood extreme heat in a full body cast and remembers how he told his boss not to beat up the old drunk who was bothering Doc because the old drunk was Doc's father, and he knew him, and his ways.

And I respect Doc, and his tragedies, and his simple life.

My Shit-Stained Friend Who Exists On Smoke Alone

I am eating by myself and understanding the concept of eating everything on one's plate because I don't know when my next meal will be.

Behind me, this one woman approaches another woman and offers her three egg rolls. The woman accepts them. She is dressed very well and looks very well-fed and looks very healthy. She places the three egg rolls right next to her already full plate of rice, beef and broccoli, and chow mein. She adds the three egg rolls to all of this and continues to feed her face while drinking from a large cup of soda.

Another woman passes my view. I have seen her before because she approached me yesterday and apologized for being nosy and asked me about my work. And I told her. And she nodded while taking a drag from her cigarette and then squinted through one eye when exhaling it. And I explained to her unwashed hair, and I explained to her bra-less boobs, and I explained to her dirty shoes. And she nodded and smoked and apologized again for being so nosy, turned, and walked away.

She's now passing my view. She is smoking a cigarette with one squinted eye again and conversing with an equally strange-looking man. She passes by very quickly. Well, quicker than I ever imagined her form could carry her. I believe that she exists on cigarettes and casual conversation alone.

I make a new observation about her that I didn't notice yesterday. She is wearing the same clothes: an old hooded zipper jacket, and the same thin T-shirt with her bra-less breasts still exposed, and out of her shoes I can see her dirty toes, but I notice something else which completes the whole outfit. A series of shit stains can be seen through the back of her jeans. And I think, *Oh man, how obscene.*

I feel sorry for her. I wish that I could share some of my food with her, but I am too hungry myself. I question in my mind why the woman with the three unwanted egg rolls would give them to a well-fed and well-bred woman who obviously doesn't need them. Those three egg rolls would have been better appreciated by my shit-stained friend who exists on smoke alone.

Quit Running and Embrace the Madness

Why try to set a date? Why even bother trying?

Because all that will ever happen is "change" will punch you square in the face and change that date and maybe even your state.

Why bother running from the madness?

I had been running for a long time until I found it easier to stop dead in my tracks, turn around, throw out my arms, and have madness catch up with me. It slammed into my being, possessed me in a strange embrace, and knocked me flat on my back. And then, I started laughing.

I looked up at the clouds and watched them rush by. And watched the occasional plane. And watched the sun and the day. And watched the moon and the night. And I laughed at the madness that filled my whole being. And it felt pretty damn good.

I gathered myself together and pushed myself up off the ground and started walking in some direction. I was without dates, and without time, and without knowing or caring.

In insanity and in sanity I continue to carry myself towards somewhere. Towards something. Towards someone.

BLANK BOOK THREE

March

Okay, We'll Be Friends Then

I sit alone, away from the bustle of traffic, like a parked car on the side of a highway. I ponder the course, the course which people zoom through and around. I sit alone and smile as rare feelings fill me.

I think of only one who fills me up with happiness and thoughts of beauty. It was just recently that the only thoughts which consumed me when I thought of her were her body and her surprising maturity contained in her young form. Thoughts of her large hazel eyes. Thoughts of her big full lips and the way her face lit up when she parted those big full lips and revealed an infectious smile. A smile that could stop me cold. And a laugh that made me feel old. Other thoughts made me feel like a dirty old man because I would just imagine what I would do to her with only my hand.

It all came around to last night. I was overwhelmed with emotion and I asked her point-blank what she thought of me. And she told me. My anger was brief. And so was my sadness.

She called me an ass, and I felt like an ass. I said, "Let's go," like an asshole. In silence, we moved angrily towards the door. She went first and I went second. In my mad and sad state, I stopped and said, "Stop, please, come back." And in her mature youthful form, she came back to me. We embraced and it felt warm. I said, "Let's talk about it." We went back in and faced each other on the couch. And suddenly, I understood all, and the placement of us on that couch at that time. It all hit me very suddenly. I looked at her large hazel eyes and her beautiful lips and tears accumulated on the bottoms of my eyes, but they did not fall, merely welled at the rims. And she needed me and I needed her. And she needed me and I needed her. And then we embraced and were one in a much-needed friendship. The two of us now one.

A moment, like a tear welling at the rim.

We came to realize a much more beautiful union than just sex and physical pleasure. Don't get me wrong, that union would be grand, but it would likely be short-lived. And now I can truly say without a hint or a promise or a lie, "I love you." I am happy about the weight of my heart filled with the beauty of our union transcending.

Decadence and Decay Every Day

I am sitting on a bench that I thought was removed from the hustle and bustle of everyday life. I thought I had removed myself from the decadence and decay that always seems to find me. I sit and try to write, as I have been trying to do often, but I always manage to get interrupted by something.

I am forcing my pen and trying to put my feelings to paper through the lifelessness of dead black plastic.

Even if I try to make up things to write about, I quickly realize, why bother? No matter how removed, no matter how much I move, my path is a crash course for decadence, an intersection for decay.

Decadence and decay cross my path every day. My path of trying to put the everything of the everyone into some kind of perspective and meaning.

Why should I force the writing? I just need to change my direction and wait. The words will come and write themselves if I just wait for them to come.

Anyway, I was just sitting there, trying to force the words out of my pen and coax them onto the paper, when I notice a large black man on crutches approaching my periphery. He stops and swings around and sits down next to me.

I slowly close my dead book and return my dead pen back to my pocket. I turn and open my ear to the inevitable and the unbelievable and I say very casually, "So, tell me what happened."

And then he starts gushing forth, like a cork released from a champagne bottle.

"Well," he begins, "just yesterday I was at a friend's house and I was on the second floor and somehow the house caught on fire and I leaped out the window and fucked up my ankle."

"How much longer?" I ask.

"The doctor says four more days on the crutches and then a couple of days in an air splint and all this after just spending $700 on a doctor's bill from a visit a couple of weeks ago."

"What happened then?"

"I was stepping off the Metro and managed to step right into a shootout. I went ducking and I got hit in the meaty part of my forearm. It passed right through."

I say, "That's a fucked-up Metro stop. Which one was it? I'll try to avoid it."

He laughs.

I then say, "By the way, my name's Greg."

We shake hands.

"I'm Carl."

"Well, Carl, I have got to get back to work now, my break is over. Try to keep the faith, my friend. And try to avoid fucked-up Metro stops."

"Peace."

I move back towards work and feel frustrated because I didn't get any writing done on my break.

Between Every Fuck and Piss Time Passes

I was having a great day. Everything was going well. But, everything was so fucking deceiving.

Work passed quickly and all I did was debate in my mind whether to partake in a poetry slam that night.

People were saying, "Do it. You might win and be able to buy more drinks and some food."

So I sat, sober, and tried to decide which poems I would read. I imagined myself winning and I was suddenly happy that I might be able to fill my stomach AND be able to pay for it.

So, I went, and I was filled with a lot of anticipation.

And everything was still going well and I arrived in one piece and I signed up and I was one of twelve that signed up, and eight were to be chosen from a hat to compete, and I thought, *No problem. Everything is going well.*

But, everything was so fucking deceiving.

I was not chosen, but I was not upset because Rolling Rocks were only one dollar. Until I went for a second and was informed that, "Happy Hour is now over. Two dollars and fifty cents, please."

"Fuck."

My friend was there, her name is January.

My other friend was there, his name is not. It just simply is.

And let me mention that to become sufficiently buzzed enough to think what I write was worth reading, I did two shots of vodka and slammed two Rolling Rocks and, fuck, I was not even chosen.

Well, I still had January and my other not-named-after-a-month friend and everything was still okay, but everything was so fucking deceiving.

Even though I was not chosen, I was still excited to hear something that I had never heard before. Maybe something that someone could tell me, teach me, help me find my way.

But, I should have known, most people are so fucking unenlightening.

Fuck.

I met another girl through January and she seemed very interesting, but shy, so, nothing.

I saw another girl who I recognized but could not place and I thought, *Fuck. She is so cute. If only I could remember who she is.*

I sat through reader after reader after reader, unenlightened and bored.

Fuck.

I know I would have made it through the first round and the second, but no, I was not chosen among the eight from only twelve. Among the eight from only twelve!

Fuck.

January cuts out early because she only came in hopes that I would read because she hasn't seen or heard from me in a month and a week. I stopped her before she left and she stooped down and kissed me and suddenly, everything started going well again.

The moisture from her lips still lingered on my lips. And that was all I really needed, to know that I was still worth kissing.

I was suddenly revitalized and brave.

I went to the bathroom and filled an empty beer glass with my piss in hopes that one of tonight's performers would find it and think it's a free beer.

I only later thought that I hope my non-month-named friend did not discover it and become deceived first.

I hope that one of those desperate readers discovered it first. Desperate for words. Desperate to be heard. And desperate for a warm fucking beer, as desperate as I was to be kissed.

I made a phone call to a friend in hopes that it might lead to something else and, "Yes," she said, "pick me up in half an hour."

And once again everything was going well, but everything was so fucking deceiving.

I went back to my seat next to my non-month-named friend because I still had some time and I still had enough patience to search for some meaning that I could apply to my up-and-down life.

Nope. I was still bored and sat without understanding.

But, my friend who I recognized approached me. She said, "Didn't I meet you at that coffeehouse last week?"

And I said, "Yes."

And I thought, *Yes! Now I remember. God, I want you. Fuck, you are so young.*

Everything was so fucking deceiving.

Even the body of youth can seem so fucking mature. *Fuck, I feel so old. Damn, I want you.*

Anyway, I thought about the potential-for-furthermore friend I had phoned and soon left. I said "Goodbye" to my non-month-named friend and my newly-met-shy friend and the didn't-recognize-but-now-remember-and-want-to-hump friend. And I left the suffocating words of the those-who-don't-know-any-better writers or, at least, the nothing-I-can-use writers.

Fuck.

I drove to the potential-for-furthermore friend and found

out that she could no longer go out. We fought in the rain in the parking lot and I returned to my car and was reminded by my one and only functional windshield wiper that I was alone and that no one shared the seat next to me.

Fuck.

I drove home.

I did a shot of vodka and stewed about how everything was so fucking deceiving tonight.

And I drank another shot to that fact alone.
And I drank another shot to that fact... alone.

I then went out again because the night was still young.

Fuck.

Lip and Lung Love of the Semi-Limbless Kind

It's about time that I write about the man who has no arms cut off just above his elbows.

I have seen him twice now.

The first time I saw him, I thought, *What could be worse than having no arms cut off just above the elbows?* And then, he showed me.

He is a smoker.
He is addicted to nicotine.

I saw him squeeze a cigarette between his two nubs and thrust his head forward to take a hit, and I wondered, *How in the hell did he get that cigarette lit?* And, isn't it a bitch to have no arms and then be addicted to nicotine? Or worse, be addicted to nicotine and then lose your arms. Now that would be one strung-out dude. But, I bet he learned real fast how to light and smoke a cigarette with just two nubs and one mouth because he is addicted to nicotine and, isn't life a bitch?

It's hard to look real cool with no arms AND a bad habit.

When I saw him the second time, I watched real close.

He shook loose a cigarette from his pack with both nubs. And then he nubbed that cigarette up and placed it between his two lips. He then nubbed a strike-anywhere match and nubbed it into an anywhere surface. He lifted that lit match with both nubs to his one cigarette held between his two lips and then he sucked that lit match into his cigarette. He blew out the match with one breath and released it from between his two nubs into a nearby trash can. He then nubbed his lit cigarette to death.

With black on the ends of his nubs, and black on the insides of his lungs, and black thoughts filling his head about being armless and a smoker.

A Dude and Some Drunk Bitch

A dude with a fat belly and nothing else leans against a pillar in the bar.

On stage, two older-looking long-hairs strum the shit out of their acoustic guitars and try to strum sex through their instruments and try to spit sex through their microphones and try to get sex from some drunk bitch who is convinced that the two long-hairs are half of Spinal Tap.

Spinal Tap is her favorite movie.

So she spreads her legs for the sex of instruments and microphones and is so convinced that they're half of Spinal Tap that she spreads her legs anyway.

She says to me, "Aren't they geniuses?"

"No."

"Sure they are, they're half of Spinal Tap."

"No, they're not."

"Sure they are."

"No, they are not."

"Sure they are."

"Okay," I lie. "You're right, they are."

"See. I told ya."

Meanwhile, the other half of Spinal Tap is being born in the fat belly of the dude leaning against the pillar, and he has nothing else but Spinal Tap in his belly and.... *What the fuck am I talking about?*

Who cares. I knew I shouldn't have come here.

Too many old long-hairs and fat fucks trying to get laid, and trying to lay it into chicks who are easily impressed by dudes who look like half of Spinal Tap.

Her and I

What? I hear you.
I know I need to write about her.

But, nothing.
But, blank.

She said, "I love you." And, "I need you."

And I, nothing.
And I, blank.

All I could merely do was hug her in the rain, and kiss her hair, as she sobbed against my chest.

I said, "Another time, another time. I'm sorry. This isn't right.

"You've had some drinks, and I've had some drinks, so let's don't. Let's not. This isn't right. Not like this. This isn't right. Another time. Another time. I'm sorry.

"It would be so easy to say, 'Yes, I need you,' and, 'Yes, I love you too.' But no, this isn't right.

"Another time. Another time, perhaps."

Sharing Spaces and Thinking

I enjoy being up 20 hours out of each day. Each hour awake is an hour that doesn't seem lost.

I think about how we move between new spaces and familiar spaces and how we meet new people and see the same old people and how we manage to feel good even when feeling bad and how we are constantly interacting with people who are either feeling good or feeling bad and how we understand that, in that moment, we are sharing the same space and the same time, together. In some room, somewhere, during some time, for that moment, alone. That act of sharing seems special, good or bad.

I was sharing some space last night with a friend and we were drinking vodka shots and beer and talking with my roommate who wasn't drinking for the first time since I met him because he had two mid-terms the next day. And we talked. And we drank. And we talked about drinking and drugs while watching *Cops* and seeing people get busted for selling or doing drugs. And we talked. And we drank. And we talked. And eventually my roommate went to sleep.

So, now time passed and the space shifted and it was just me and my friend. We mourned bad timing and ill-timed placement of our beings in space. And we wished and we drank. And we touched and were lying in each other's arms. And we mourned and felt the pain of what-ifs and what-could-have-beens. And we caressed each other in ill-timed, ill-placed pain. I then drove her to her boyfriend's.

After I dropped her off, I moved on to an old, familiar space and saw some of the same old people. I talked to these same people in old familiarity and, in happiness, we mourned the pain which reminds us that we are human and alive. I lost track of time and left at closing.

I moved back to my space and watched *Love Connection* and mourned the pain until it passed. The show ended and I moved into bed and slept. I slept without dreaming because I only slept for four hours. I hate missing a thing.

I picked up my friend who I just dropped off six hours earlier and we looked at each other with wet hair and heavy eyelids and we laughed. She lit a cigarette and I drove her to her first gynecological exam, and I drove her to "my" first gynecological exam, and if I really stopped to think about this… but I don't. I don't like missing a thing.

I did 80 from Fairfax to Springfield and made good time and the only thing I tried to miss were all the cars I was moving around. And, did I mention my stomach? How I could drive with just vodka and beer and so much buttered toast that I could shit a loaf, I don't know. But right now my empty stomach and my empty head and all the empty bottles and all the empty cans and all the empty cars and all the empty spaces were waiting with time to be filled, spaces with nothing but time waiting to be filled, space and time, waiting to be filled.

I moved quickly down the highway to get to that gynecology office just so I could fill it and just so it would be another shared space that I would be spending time in with my friend. Sharing her first gynecology exam, but not sharing her gynecology.

She went in.

I sat in the waiting area and thought, *What the hell am I doing here?* I wished I could fill my empty stomach because my empty head needed something.

While sitting there, I couldn't help but think about vaginas and what it must be like to be a woman. I couldn't stop thinking about all the blood involved with every month's period. The idea of being reminded of one's sexuality when bleeding in the bathtub while showering or when sitting on the toilet to piss and seeing blood. It seemed warped. A man is reminded of his sexuality by squeezing a much more pleasant deposit into the bathtub or toilet. Or, if he's lucky, into someone's vagina. Or into someone's mouth. Or into someone's ass. Or onto someone's chest. This reminder seems preferable to the reminder of one's sexuality through bloody deposits.

And then I thought, *I need to spend more time sleeping instead of awake and thinking like this.*

She finally came out. She was a little shaken up, but still in one piece (I guess). She finished her paperwork and we left.

I was running out of time to get to my work space, so, we hopped in my car and moved quickly again around others. I asked her how it was. She said, "Okay."

Then, there was silence.

A song by The Doors started playing on the radio. *"There's blood in the streets, it's up to my ankle/ There's blood in the streets, it's up to my knees."* I thought, *Through that song, Morrison must have been trying to imagine life from a woman's point of view.*

Some time passed. A couple of miles passed under the car. In our mobile, shared space, I turned and asked her if she wanted to talk about it. But she confused my question with a query to revisit our discussion of the night before. That's the last thing I wanted to do was reawaken that pain of what-could-have-been.

I said, "No, I mean, about the exam. Do you want to talk about the exam?"

She said, "Well, he would tell me everything he was doing, like, 'Now I am putting my finger in there and now…,' whatever and whatever, until he was done."

I tried to make light of an otherwise awkward and painful experience and said, "Well, that helps. You wouldn't want him shoving fruit up there without letting you know first."

Her serious face broke and she burst out laughing.

I continued, pretending to be the doctor, "We are going to try a new exam I am developing called, 'Identify the Fruit.' I am going to place fruit into your vagina and I want you to tell me what it is. Ready? Begin. Okay, so that one was easy. Yes, that was a banana. Try this one.

Good, good. Yes, that was a kiwi. Here, try this one. Oh, I'm sorry, did that hurt? You guessed correctly, that was a cantaloupe."

And she laughed. And I laughed. And the miles moved beneath my car. I dropped her off at home and told her to take it easy. I raced off to work, barely in time to open.

Reality brought me back around to sobriety when I went to wash my hands in the public restroom. I found myself sharing the same time and space with a man I was observing in the mirror. He was at the urinal and he had dropped his pants and his underwear down to his knees. His bare ass was staring at me from beneath his windbreaker and I thought, *God I love being awake 20 hours out of 24.* I do not want to miss the reality of a man who hasn't refined his pissing skills enough to use a public urinal, and doesn't care, and shows the world his bare ass from beneath his windbreaker.

I left that bathroom thinking about how good it was to be alive and how good my stomach would feel when I filled it with a sausage and egg biscuit from Roy Rogers. Or, was it now Hardees breakfast in Roy Rogers? Did Roy Rogers buy Hardees? Oh, who gave a fuck. It was an old and familiar space, and I was alive, and I loved it.

What am I Like?

You ask me what I am like
and I will tell you.

I enjoy driving in my car
really fast.

I like pushing the accelerator
through every turn
while everyone else
is applying their brakes.

It makes the curves
seem really straight
when I step on the gas
and speed through a curve.

I do most of my passing
during a turn or a curve
because I accelerate
while everyone else brakes.

Bukowski and Me
(March 9, 1994)

"Bukowski is dead."

Those words hit me and I immediately denied them.

"What?"

"Bukowski is dead."

"Fuck you."

"No really, he died on Wednesday."

"Fuck you. You're kidding, right?"

"No. He is dead."

Fuck. Fuck.

That fucking bastard.

I didn't even get to meet him. I didn't even get to meet him drunk. I didn't even get to meet him and buy him a beer and nothing else. Not even a word. Just a beer bought and a beer shared and maybe a cigarette or two. But, no. That motherfucker had to die.

Fuck. I am sad.

It was him, Charles Bukowski. Not Frost. Not Pound. Not Stevens. Not Williams. Not Keats. Not Yeats. Not

Cummings. Not Dickinson. None of them. They all frustrated me and frightened me from the written word. No, it was Chuck Buk, that crazy motherfucker.

It was only two months ago that he inspired me to love the written word, and practice and try, and try and practice. I read six of his books of poetry and I lived him and I loved him. Like a father. Like a mentor. Like a teacher. And now, my deity has died.

He left me with no wings. Just a pen and a paper and a pain. A pain for thoughts. A pain for words. A pain for beer.

It was only a couple of weeks ago that I wanted to call him because I knew his phone number would be listed. But, I didn't. I remembered reading one of his poems which advised to leave the dead to their dying. So, I hesitated and I didn't call. I didn't even think about writing him a letter because I have a hard enough time writing for myself now. A letter would have been even more painful. Besides, I wouldn't know what to say either way. Besides, I was counting on crossing his path one day and, whatever. You know, whatever.

But now, old Chuck Buk is dead. Fuck.

I return to this book and squeeze ink from this pen, like I imagine he squeezed sperm from his dick. I drink beer and do vodka shots to his benefit, postmortem. I think about how it has been a month since the last book of his poetry that I read because I only had time for my own writing after he inspired me.

The words that I needed to say were suddenly a shitstorm in my brain that I had to get out.

Now, I look at how nicely his books make coasters for my beer. I know that he would have preferred things to continue this way. With shots dedicated to him. And pussy on the brain. And beer resting on his books of poetry, as I imagine a beer clutched within his hand right now, buried.

Fuck you, Chuck Buk, you old dead bastard. I love you, man.

I think it's important to pause and dedicate a "fuck you" to the dead who inspired you, because they at least deserve that. And one day, Chuck Buk, I will drink a beer near your grave, and I will probably deposit that same beer on top of your head.

Bastard.

12 Bucks and Almost a Free Pack of Cigarettes

I am consumed with the fact that I have no money.

I am waiting for my next paycheck as I clutch ten dollars in the form of two fives to my chest. I blow three bucks on breakfast and five bucks plus on lunch.

I managed to survive all weekend on ham and cheese sandwiches, and turkey and cheese sandwiches, and salami and cheese sandwiches. On sandwiches, sandwiches, and sandwiches. Mustard and mayo, mayo and mustard. And thank God for my charitable roommate for a twelve-pack of Milwaukee's Best and half a bottle of vodka. I got drunk and forgot all about the fact that only two fives existed in my wallet.

Now, I only have one dollar and some change left.

After I get off work, I wander around Retail Hell and imagine that I have a pocketful of money and a charge card with no limit. I start buying things in my mind. And I continue to wander, even after I have checked out and I wonder why, as I wander by. And then, all is answered when, I discover a ten dollar bill and two ones in my path.

I think, *Right on! My luck is changing.*

I pick up the ten and two ones and I leave Retail Hell where one store has a picture of its owners adorning the front door. I wonder how they make any sales when people with little money enter and see where their little money gets spent, on the fuckers whose picture adorns the front door. Rich millionaires! And those who enter who are not. Putting their hard-earned cash into the store owners' pockets and turning their now empty pockets inside out.

Bad marketing move, that photograph, I think. *They don't give enough credit to their thinking consumers.*

But, with twelve dollars in my pocket, I feel rich.

I think, *Now I can buy some cigarettes and some breakfast and some lunch tomorrow, after a dinner tonight of a turkey and mayo and cheese sandwich.*

There is still no paycheck, but I feel rich. No photograph of mine adorns a window.

I leave Retail Hell feeling lucky. I go to my car and spy a pack of cigarettes on the dashboard of the car next to mine. I check to see if any of the doors are unlocked. No, I am not that lucky. But I know I shouldn't get greedy, with twelve bucks and almost a pack of cigarettes. For free.

I put off stealing from my job another day, because I have twelve bucks and a turkey and mayo and cheese sandwich on my mind, and almost a free pack of cigarettes.

Almost.

I Hate It When

I hate it when my ashtray gets emptied
because the bartender just does not understand
the goal of a filled ashtray.

Fuck!

Now I have to start over and I am pissed,
pissed that I have to start the whole fucking project
over again.

And now the bastard acoustic player sings
"Stormy Weather."

And I think of a girl I know,
and how beautifully her version of that song kicks his
ass because this motherfucker has never experienced
"Stormy Weather," but sings it anyway.

Fuck the bitch bartender
and the bastard acoustic player
who both don't know

about the triumph of tragedy and decay
in a song and in an ashtray.

Superball

I love my superball. It saves me from the confines of boredom's walls. I just pull out my superball and follow it wherever it goes. And when I get tired of bouncing it, I hold it between my thumb and index finger and look at its colors. Green. Green-blue. White. And red. It looks like a watermelon exploded on a picnic ground. There's no sign of people, they must have all scattered after the watermelon exploded.

When I tire of imagining the picnic gone bad, I think about all the superballs I must have had when I was a kid. Most trips to the grocery store with my mom yielded some-sized superball from the coin-operated vending machines. But, it was only in my hand for a few seconds.

As soon as we got outside, I would raise that superball high up over my head, and throw it down into the ground as hard as I could. And, for one glorious moment, that ball would bounce high in the sky, pause there, and come hurtling back down to Earth. And then it would bounce off in some strange direction that I couldn't possibly anticipate. I would watch it bound away from me and into traffic and that would be it.

My mom would say, "Leave it. It's gone. I told you not to do that. Haven't you learned yet?"

But that was exactly what I wanted to do with it when I had it. Its life was short-lived, but how glorious that one superball's moment was, pausing so high in the sky.

Well, my new superball, with its watermelon explosion, is special. It's special because I was sitting somewhere recently and it just rolled up into view and stopped at my foot. I picked it up and looked around to see if some child would be scrambling after it, but I knew better.

On the other side of this ball was some gleeful kid with a huge smile on his face. And that made me smile. And, to me, of all the lost superballs of my childhood, here was one finding its way back to me. This one represented them all.

I have managed to hold on to this superball for over two months now, even after bouncing it three hundred thousand times. And maybe one day, I will try to recapture the glory and send this superball flying.

But not today.

And I Feel That Time's A Wasted

"And I feel, and I feel/ When the dogs begin to smell her/ Will she smell alone?"

I raced in my car to a poetry slam and I have decided that poetry slams were not meant for me. I went to a poetry slam instead of doing what I really wanted to be doing on St. Patrick's Day and that was drink beer.

I sat in a café in Georgetown, waiting for time to arrive at the moment of poetry slamming, but, not enough people showed up, so, "There will be no poetry slam tonight, only a poetry reading."

Damn.

So, I waited. I found myself writing something inane about a superball and I smoked cigarettes, because I was nervous, because I was sober, because I hate being nervous about reading my shit, sober. I should have followed my initial instinct, I should have kept my books closed and went and got drunk, but no, Bukowski is still dead and I died under the light, behind a microphone, while sitting in a chair, sober.

I raced in my car to the Safeway near home and got a 12-pack of Milwaukee's Best Light (because I am on a diet) and I stood in Harry's checkout line behind a lonely, short woman.

Harry has worked there so long, he looks like he is tenured. He's always telling me jokes. And I always laugh, but it's not at his jokes, it's at the absurdity of a fat balding man telling me dirty jokes in a Safeway checkout line. I do love him for it though.

I stood in line and found myself in pathetic eager anticipation of Harry's latest joke. Before he finished with the lady, Harry turned to me and asked if it's cold outside.

I said, "Kind of, it's pretty windy."

The woman asked if I heard about the possibility of sleet or snow.

I said, "No."

It would make sense to me, though. It's been that kind of day.

Harry said, "Yeah, a possibility of a two-inch accumulation overnight."

I said, "Thanks, it all makes sense now."

Then, the woman left.

"And I feel, so much depends on the weather"

I said to Harry, "You know, I got in your line to hear a joke, not a depressing weather report."

He brightened up, alive and on stage, and asked me what the last one he told me was.

I said, "It was the one about Lorena Bobbitt defecting to Russia."

With people in line behind me, he inched real close. I sensed secrecy in his approach. This one was going to be good.

He whispered, "What's the difference between pussy and pizza?"

I whispered back, "What?"

He whispered, "Well, you can eat the crust off a pizza."

I laughed and I laughed and I laughed at the absurdity of it all. I bellowed, "Well shit, bring on the snow! I'm in a better mood now."

Harry smiled.

I bailed with my 12-pack of Milwaukee's Best Light. I waved at the woman who was in front of me now passing me in her car. I felt a strange camaraderie.

I rushed home so I could catch up on all that drinking I missed out on this fucked-up St. Patrick's Day.

"Where ya going to tomorrow?"

Digesting Revenge

I have gone beyond hungry and have now achieved the comfortable numbness of starvation when you move past the point of absolute hunger and any desire to fill your stomach with a whole pizza, three cheeseburgers, four burritos, and a seafood buffet has now slipped into a state which leaves your eyes free-floating and your empty stomach glowing a strange warmth as it begins to digest itself.

The initial panic of hunger sends an impulse to your brain that says, "Feed me!" and you don't, because you can't, but you want to, but you can't.

Once through that initial hunger panic stage, your stomach tells your brain, "Fuck off then, I don't need you," and begins to digest itself and plans to eat your self inside out just to get back at the brain and eventually the mouth, the mouth which will not eat, the mouth which cannot eat, because there is nothing to eat.

The warmth and numbness spreads a revenge directed at your self.

I Smile at Strange Things

I smile when I see a drunken man sitting on the curb with his knees drawn up and his head bowed between his knees, and his hands placed on the back of his neck.

He is shaking his head in drunken disbelief, his car has a glowing police car parked behind it, and a cop circles around him, writing the drunken man's story on a single sheet of paper.

I smile and think how stupid he is for being drunk, sitting on a curb, next to his car, caught. Caught moments before, drunk and in his car.

Then I think, *Why do I think he is stupid for being caught?* Especially when that could have been me just the night before.

I am actually very jealous that the drunken man's life story can be reduced to a single sheet of paper.

On the other hand, I am nearing the end of my third blank book in a little over two months and I still don't have a clue. But I do know, and do not understand how, a blank book can be more expensive than one that has words. It doesn't make sense.

But it does make me smile.

I smile when I sit in AAA and think about how pissed I am at the United States Navy for taking my best friend away from me. That's going to be the title of my next shitstorm, whenever I can scrape together enough money for another blank book: "Sitting in AAA Pissed Off at the United States Navy."

I smile at getting buzzed off two vodka shots and two beers and not waking up with a headache.

I smile at the fact that extinguishing my cigarette in a urinal seems like some kind of graduation.

I smile at the day when I wake up and immediately reach for a beer for breakfast.

I smile at getting my silly hands on another blank book and filling it with cheap words.

I smile at a day's worth of dust floating atop that night's first shot of vodka.

I smile because I don't care.

I smile as I become so desperate that I am scrawling this on the blank book's back cover.

BLANK BOOK FOUR

March – April

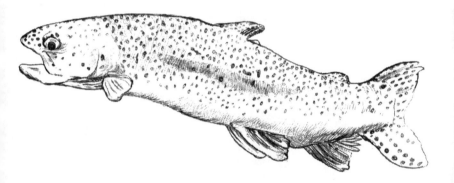

Moving Towards Some Plot

I have never been so stressed out in my life.

My organs are in an uproar, playing a violent symphony within me. It's an allegro, I think. All the violinists are plucking my nerves with pizzicato ferocity while the entire horn section waits in horrible self-containment. They're sitting in my middle with horns resting on their legs, waiting for an opportunity to turn this allegro into a bloody jamboree.

Just when I think I have it all figured out and I manage to fight the urge to abandon my car at a red light and walk away, the light turns green and I somehow proceed.

I resist quitting by blaring angry music from my car stereo that creates an almost womb-like environment in my eggshell car frame. This helps. I try concentrating on the car's destination, and then on the street's destination, and then on any destination that isn't mine, but it's no use. Reality manages to seep its way in.

I am jealous of my best friend who appears to be making a move in the right direction. I feel like I am just continuing straight ahead through a gauntlet of flying fists. I have no way to protect my face or waist as my hands are bound behind me and I'm running through the middle as fast as I possibly can.

Back to the symphony in my middle, I don't know what to do. I'm hoping it's some kind of curable chemical imbalance. I ate a decent breakfast and I drank lots of fluids. I felt the need to eat something healthy at lunch so I got a salad with my slice of pizza. And then, I got another slice of pizza. And now my symphony is really moving. It has its motivation and is moving towards some plot. Or is being pushed towards some plot. Or plot, plot, plot. No plot. Just a never-ending story with no plot.

No plot to piss in.

No plot to shit in.

Not even a plot for puking.

And I think, *Maybe I just need some sugar.* So I eat two and one-quarter cookies. And then I think, *Boy, was I stupid for thinking that what I had was a sugar deficiency.*

The symphony continues to drone on and on and on.

It's not just my best friend's move that is stressing me out. It is my ex-girlfriend. It is my job. It is my upcoming move with my job. It is my mom (not really). It is my new living situation. It is my old living situation. It is my financial situation (or lack thereof). It is beer. It is cigarettes.

It is knowing the night before that when people asked me, "Why is your shirt and part of your pants wet?" and I replied, "I spilled beer on my lap," but I had actually pissed on myself the moment before.

I had it under control. I lifted my shirtfront up and tucked it under my chin. But then, as I was pissing, the shirtfront slipped and interrupted my stream of consciousness. In fact, it passed that stream of consciousness onto the front of my pants and, "Shit! Fuck! Fuck! Shit!" as I quickly plucked the shirtfront up, but it was too late, it was soaked.

In the mirror, I squeezed the piss out of my shirt and shrugged at the piss spot on my pants.

During that, as I was standing there squeezing piss from my shirt, I came to a realization. I realized that that piss was really just a long-journeyed beer through my system and I felt like I just wasted a beer and I was feeling like I was not that far off. But, I did walk away from that scene before squeezing that beer-piss from my shirt directly into a pint glass for recycling.

(Not that desperate.) (Yet.)

And and and…

I am so stressed, but am feeling much better now, having managed to get that off my chest. And now the symphony has subsided to a buzzing that is heading for the floor and out the door.

And damn it all if the most intense and loving eyes that were directed at me belonged to a man and not my gender of choice.

And damn damn damn…

Fuck love.

Fuck work.

Fuck money and daisies.

And fuck....

Hey! She was kind of cute. She even looked in my direction. I wonder where she's going to. I wish I were going too.

And this is why I don't quit or bail from my car under the stress of a long red light. Because, patience, soon the red light will be green.

A Stream of Consciousness Writing

This guy comes up to me and says, "I've seen you read. I like your stuff."

And I think, *Calling it "stuff" seems appropriate.*

And then he says, "It's like cool, stream of consciousness poetry."

And I say, "Poetry? Is what I write poetry?" It seems very questionable to me, in my mind. What is poetry?

To me, poetry is writing about life and conveying a higher understanding about what one knows. I have read a lot of "highly-regarded" poets and heard a lot of "wannabe highly-regarded" poets and through them the whole life experience conveyance thing fails me, often.

Too many times I have read or heard poems by these "poets" and I fail to get their point, and I know that it is my failure in understanding, but I do keep trying, and I do keep writing "stuff."

I marvel at the simple, and I wonder at the everyday, and I write about "stuff."

I marvel at a child who points to a picture of the Bee Gees' Barry Gibb and says, "Jesus?"

And I wonder, *Why, why does this child think so?* And, *Why, why does this child need so?*

Why do the lessons of morality depend so heavily on a single text written a long, long, long, long time ago?

Can we not fathom the lesson and density of poetry in a simple, empty bag and the sadness that comes with it?

I marvel at the humor and the beauty of my roommate drunk off his ass as he stumbles through the door glorious. A huge grin (so big that it seems to float three feet in front of him) animates his face. He sheds his jacket to the ground in one motion and plops into a chair and begins flavoring every statement with the adjective "tremendous."

"It was a tremendous evening. It was a tremendously drunken affair. The people beside me were tremendously pissed when, in my tremendously drunken state, I purposely spilled their drinks all over the bar, because I hated them tremendously."

He then describes the friends he was with as "fishy" and soon everyone becomes "fishy" because soon everyone becomes his friend. And his tremendously fishy friends, who swim in schools, swam from their school in Tennessee, leaving one beer pool, and taking my roommate out along with them, where they went swimming from pool to pool, and it was tremendous.

And I laugh and wish that I had pen and paper to capture his every word. Because, to me, that is poetry.

Bedroom Eyes Walks By

Listen, Bedroom Eyes,
are you looking to break a heart?
Or just be near one?

Because, right now,
I just want to be near another beating heart.
Preferably yours, Bedroom Eyes.

Bedroom Eyes' Lips

Look, look, Bedroom Eyes,
why do you continue to just walk on by?

Why don't you stop and at least say, "Hi."
Or stop and say, "Bye" and continue on by.

I can see by your bedroom eyes, Bedroom Eyes,
that you crave being held by much more than just
my own blue eyes.

You demonstrate your desires by teasing and displaying
your abilities with your mouth upon a defenseless ice
cream cone while your bedroom eyes look at me,
Bedroom Eyes, and tease.

Your mouth can take in that entire ice cream cone,
I can see.

I can see that when you remove the cone of vanilla ice
cream from your mouth, your lips are outlined in white.
Your lips are outlined. Your lips. Your lips….

Damn, Bedroom Eyes, you have a beautiful set of lips.

I wish you'd part those lips for me,
if only in passing conversation.

The Old Trout

Women pass by wearing thin, short dresses with sandals or small sneakers on, and flowers in their hair.

Women pass by wearing short, tight shorts which barely hold up the bottom of their asses.

And women pass by....
And women pass by....

Reminding me of the coming of Spring and eventually Summer again.

And then the old man who works beside me covertly comes up behind me and lurks, and then trails off in some strange direction as he spins and almost falls over, but manages to move his feet fast enough to catch up with his top-heavy body.

And this man scares me.
And this man stresses me out.
Because he is like an old, aimless trout.

Nearly entirely bald, with teeth like he has had *de*constructive surgery done on his skull. These teeth tell histories of tooth decay and cigarette smoking. And the skin on his face resembles that of a burn victim.

He comes up to me with a bag of Sun Chips in his hand and is so proud of his "meal" which he explains only cost him "69 cents, or 72 cents with tax." And he also calls a coffee and a muffin a "meal" at only "$1.25, or $1.31

with tax."

And… and… and….

Swim away, Old Trout! I don't care about your trivial triumphs. You stress me out and I can't figure out why.

And maybe it's because I didn't like the way you stroked that child's hair and looked at him with a grin while his mother's attention was diverted elsewhere. Or maybe it's because you pass out little bookmarks which say "God Bless You" and "Jesus Loves You" and you explain that, "For the price of a postage stamp you can have the maker of these bookmarks send you thousands," so you can distribute them to all who need a clue and are in search of the righteous direction and must have help finding salvation, so they can be saved.

Swim away, Old Trout! You stress me out. The way you swim up behind and lurk – or the way you swim up beside and lurk. And, swim away! because you are making me look bad as all I want to do is look at dresses and short shorts and think about Spring and Summer, not look at your burn-victim face, bald head, and bestial mouth because it stresses me out.

Conversation with you is painful as all I can do is think about the possibility of a piece of Sun Chip being propelled from your mouth and landing anywhere on my face and… *Ewwwww!* Swim away, swim away, you old trout! Now you're really freaking me out! With your coffee and your cigarettes and your Sun Chips flavored sour cream and onion and the extra skin extending from the bottom of your chin and your trivial triumphs: cheap cigarettes... cheap food... cheap drink... cheap cheap, cheap cheap, cheap cheap. And all you have is this – work and cheap things, and me being a considerate and polite ear, nodding my head in fear, and I can't wait to get the hell out of here! Away from the man who licks his sour cream and onion "meal" from between his greasy fingers with a loud "SMACK! SMACK SMACK! SMACK SMACK!" and then swims over and wants to shake my hand for some trivial triumph.

Swim away, swim away, Old Trout! Please. You really, really freak me out.

I'm a Loser Baby So Why Don't You Kill Me

My head is still spinning from the night before.

I stand and lean and fear falling down in the middle of everything and everyone at work. My unwashed hair is all strung out and I can't even look up further than straight ahead because my hangover will just not allow it. I'm smiling though, because I'm thinking about last night. It's like some dreamy whirlwind that has left me spinning...

Yesterday, I left work and was concerned because I was meeting my ex-girlfriend at a coffeehouse and I had been having way too many bad experiences in coffeehouses lately, but I went there anyway because it was all way too interesting to miss. I sat in the coffeehouse and waited in nervous anticipation.

She eventually walked through the door and we embraced. She suggested we go get drinks instead and I said, "Great," because I was nervous and a drink sounded really good. We went into a nearby bar and drank. My beers were only a dollar and Zimas for her were two.

We sat and we talked and we tried to figure out where we just came from and where we were going to AND we drank and we talked and we put money in the jukebox AND we drank and we talked and it was still early AND I told her I missed her and she started stroking my back.

I became embarrassed with the thoughts that were running through my head.

She saw that and asked, "What?"

I shook my head.

She repeated, "What?"

And, while clutching my beer, I leaned over and whispered in her ear, "I want to fuck you so bad."

And she whispered back, "Me, too."

So, she and me downed her Zima and my beer and we quickly moved right out of that bar. We got in my car and raced to 7-Eleven for a couple of condoms.

She then directed me to one street and, just as I was about to park, I noticed a face in a window that was looking in our direction. I moved on to another street and parked at a dead end. We both moved to the back seat and began ripping our clothes off because we hadn't had it in weeks and, wouldn't you know? A car pulled right up behind us. Somehow, I managed to not only park at a dead end, but I parked in such a way that I was partially blocking this person's driveway and they were behind us waiting. I pulled up my pants, kind of, and climbed to the front, exposing my ass to those who were waiting.

I moved to another location and parked right in the middle of an empty street. It was there where we had better luck. Not a car went by while we fucked and we fucked and we fucked each other's backs straight. I had never done it in a car before and had always wanted to. I came and she came at least four times and it felt so fucking great and the lights were still on and the car was still running and my stereo was playing Beck.

"I'm a loser, baby, so why don't you kill me"

I abandoned the back seat going straight out the door, with one pant leg in and everything else not in, my other leg, my ass, my genitalia with a filled condom hanging from it and I soon stripped that off and flung it over my car and into the bushes with one quick flick of my wrist. I pulled up my pants and left one of my shoes in the back seat and drove us back to the bar.

We walked towards the bar and we embraced and we both felt really great. We decided that we should have broken up a long time ago because our sex had never been better. We got back to the bar and ordered a three-dollar pitcher.

Afterwards, she wanted me to spend the night and I wanted to spend the night, so, we left.

I followed her back to her place, which used to be our place, and we fucked some more just for old time's sake. And then we fell asleep in each other's arms.

She left in the morning before me. I got up soon after and walked around her place, which used to be our place, and I admired what she did with her place, which used to be our place, but always seemed to be more like her place anyway.

I downed a Vitamin C with a glass of Diet Pepsi. I ate a blueberry bagel with some cream cheese. I took a shower, but didn't wash my hair. I brushed my teeth with her toothbrush. I applied Secret Solid to my armpits and an annoying commercial slogan invaded my beleaguered brain. I drank two glasses of water and put on the same clothes as yesterday. I pulled out a book of matches from my shirt's front pocket, which I don't remember putting there.

I thought about last night and I smiled and I grinned.

I walked through her apartment door and left it locked behind me without a key to unlock it. I walked through the apartment building's back door and left it locked behind me without a key to unlock it. I got in my car and I started it up and from the stereo played...

"I'm a loser, baby, so why don't you kill me"

And, fuck, I couldn't stop smiling.

Trying to Find the Equilibrium

Well, here I am at work again trying to find the equilibrium inside myself that will allow me to endure another customer.

I am wearing the same clothes as yesterday. My hair still hasn't been washed. I can smell the Secret Solid every time I raise my arms and I feel that I am pH unbalanced.

An occasional fit of beer sweats creeps up on me as my body is trying to get rid of all the beer I consumed any way that it can. Every pore on my body periodically opens and drains.

I feel like I can't wipe my ass enough even though there is nothing there. I almost just shove some toilet paper between my two ass cheeks and leave it there, but I resist the urge to do that.

I feel that I need food so I eat so much turkey I could shit a Butterball. I then eat so many Altoids to cover up my turkey breath that I could probably shit a "curiously strong" peppermint Butterball.

And I still haven't reached my equilibrium.

One customer stresses me out so much when she asks me a simple question, I draw and shoot a beer-sweating blank.

And I drink water. And I drink more water. And I drink even more water thinking that I need to clean my system out, but I know I should just reach for Drano instead.

Suddenly, I am surrounded by police officers and I don't know why. I think, *Are they here to take me away?* And then I think, *I hope they're here to take me away.*

The rather large officer with black bags under his eyes asks me, "Did you call for assistance?"

I say, "I wish it were that easy. But, no, I did not call for assistance."

He says, "Someone called and said that a man in a white shirt needs assistance."

And I think, *Oh, that's fucking brilliant. You are looking for a man in a white shirt and you come up and surround me and scare the shit out of me and now I must go wipe my ass again. I wish I had shoved that toilet paper between my butt cheeks and left it there.*

They leave and approach another man in a white shirt.

Then, I have a brilliant idea, as I struggle to remain standing without tilting to the left. I can't even sit down without feeling like I will tilt to the left, tip over, and fall to the floor while I sweat a keg of beer and shit a peppermint Butterball.

My brilliant idea is to add coffee to the little party that is happening inside me.

And somehow, that works. I have achieved equilibrium.

Next time, I'll just go straight for the coffee.

Fucking with the Drunk Poet Drunk and Sober

1.
I walk into a coffeehouse drunk, because I have a problem. I need to be in a place that serves alcohol, but I also need to be in a place that serves creativity and imagination.

And, maybe, I should just keep my problem to myself.

I walk into a coffeehouse drunk and everybody in there knows it because everybody in there knows me. They each take their turn playing with the drunk, talking with the drunk, and generally just fucking with the drunk.

I sit there and wait for the poetry to happen. And, oftentimes, it does. Because all these young "wannabe 21s" and "wannabe-in-a-bar-right-now" come up to me, wired on caffeine, and want to tell the drunk their story.

And I listen. And I listen too well. And I write.

2.
I walk into work sober (I have to be sober in order to function at work) and I get attacked on a day that I didn't have to be at work until four in the afternoon.

I wasn't ready for what I walked into because everyone else has been here since at least 9:30 this morning and they are just waiting for something to happen... and it does... and, unfortunately, it happens to be me.

And, kind of like at the coffeehouse, everybody at work likes to fuck with the drunk poet sober.

I allow the poetry to create itself.

I walk into work with my arms full of merchandise and immediately get attacked by three people: my fellow young worker, the Taiwanese entrepreneur, and, of course, the old trout.

My fellow young worker begins by kicking me in the shins. I question why I tolerate such abuse and then I look at her beautiful face and I answer my own question.

I busy myself unloading all the merchandise and make two more trips to my car and back and they are waiting for me each time.

The Taiwanese entrepreneur says, "Why you bring in this T-shirt design? It not going to sell."

I say, "Sure it will. Nobody has seen it before and they will all think it's new."

She throws her hand up in the air and turns her face in disgust and utters a "tuhh" and walks away having delivered her blow verbally.

My fellow young worker continues kicking at my shins and stepping on my toes and punching me in the arms and stuffing trash in my front pocket just so she can pull the leg hairs out of my legs through inside my front pocket and, "Ow, ow! What the fuck are you doing?"

Then the old trout swims over his abuse. Just his presence is abuse as he lingers overhead.

He says, "I thought you said you were going to try to look better today than you did yesterday, but you actually look worse today. And you sure did look really bad yesterday."

He swims away having delivered his blow mentally.

I throw everything down, point at each of them, and yell, "I am going to kill each and every one of you. I am going to kill you and then you and then you. I am going to strike you all dead right where you're standing."

They all laugh in unison because they have caught me up to speed in a matter of minutes all the shit that has built up within them over the course of six and a half hours.

And they laugh because they know they are fucking with the drunk poet sober. They get enjoyment out of pushing all my buttons.

They go back to what they were doing, but continue to wait for an opening, an opening to deliver more blows.

I bend over to slice open the empty box with scissors and collapse it, but I find myself slicing open the backs of my fingers instead. And because nothing goes unnoticed in the middle of a mall, everyone laughs and laughs and laughs at the idiocy of me slicing open the backs of my fingers with the scissors.

Some days I just wish someone would walk right up to

me and bury a bullet in my head.

But, no. People know. And they help me along in strange ways.

Hookers and Pimps

And her long, stockinged legs sit atop the bar stool
and she winks.

Meanwhile, a black figure leans against the brick side
of a 7-Eleven and waits.

And she winks.
And he waits.

And they are both… loveless.
Winking and waiting.

Eyeballs Are Like Chewing Gum

The Christian Blonde informs me and my Taiwanese friend that she read about a woman entering a church and plucking out her eyes and she wants to know if this is possible.

I say, "Well, if she had really long fingernails…."

The Blonde twists her face in disgust and the Taiwanese laughs.

Then I say, "But she probably removed them with a melon baller."

This really disgusts the Blonde and the Taiwanese laughs harder.

The Blonde says, "I'll tell you what, I am no longer hungry for a slice of pizza with mushrooms. I can just imagine the texture of the mushrooms being similar to that of an eyeball."

The Taiwanese smiles, "No, eyes are very crunchy."

And she meant to say "chewy" like gum, but her mistake seems more fun because now the Blonde gives up this conversation altogether and is sorry she even brought it up.

The Taiwanese continues, "In Taiwan, they take eyes of pig and eyes of fish, and then they boil them, and then they dry them, and then they sell them as a snack."

I add, "And they remove them from the skulls with a melon baller."

The Blonde has had quite enough.

I shrug and say, "Well, you asked."

Now the Blonde is disgusted and the Taiwanese is hungry.

Later in the day, three men approach and ask the Christian Blonde where they can get some "greasy fried chicken" and act so strangely that it seems they are trying to provoke some kind of reaction from a petite Blonde Christian woman just by mentioning "greasy fried chicken" to her.

After they leave, I can tell she's a little shaken by the exchange, so I walk over and tell her that she should have armed herself with a melon baller. She rolls her eyes at me and snickers.

She still hasn't eaten today.

And I Sniff My Right Hand's Middle Finger

And I sniff my right hand's middle finger and it smells of musk de la pussy, de la soul, de la hole.

And it smells so strong and unfamiliar. And it smells. And I begin to sweat. I sweat because that pussy smell is so strong and unfamiliar.

And that must have been the best blow job ever, if only I could come. And she worked it, and she worked it, and she worked it, not once, but twice, and still I could not come for that pussy which smells so strong.

And it was the most experienced blow job I had ever experienced, and it felt so fucking good that I wanted to shoot a wad so hard into her mouth it would make her head explode.

And, fuck, I wanted my head to explode, but it wouldn't. And so, it didn't. Even though that was the best blow job I ever had, working my head, working my shaft, working my balls, until I lost all feeling in the tips of my fingers and they tingled. Until I lost all feeling in my face and it tingled. And, fuck, if I couldn't make my cock tingle.

But I know that was the best blow job ever. And I didn't even come.

Corporate Takeover

It all seems so simple.

A well-tailored suit and a clean haircut.

And keeping your back straight, and your tie straight, and the glasses on your face straight.

Then, you too can be looking over jewelry with a well-tailored skirt suit in high heels that tighten those black-stockinged calves, and ruby-red manicured acrylic fingernails, and a suitably stylish hairstyle.

Looking over diamonds and emeralds and choosing… whatever. Price doesn't matter.

If only I could keep my back straight and fly straight and stay straight. *Oh, dire straits.* I'm not really interested in any of that shit. I say, fuck dying straight.

I'd rather get those high heels straight up in the air, wrinkle that well-tailored skirt suit, spread apart those black-stockinged legs, fuck her until her back arches up, pull out, and then come all over her face.

The Old Trout (II)

The old trout with his simple pleasures swims over with a coffee in his hand and tells me that, "This beverage does not just have coffee, but chocolate and cinnamon as well."

And I, struggling to have something resembling a conversation, say, "It sounds like that should be served up with a spoon."

And... nothing. Not even a chuckle. Not even a break in the expression on his face. He just spins around and swims away, sipping at his "meal."

He floats over later and says, "Tell me if this sounds good for a midnight snack."

"Okay."

"A BLT."

"A what?"

"A BLT."

"Okay. Sounds pretty good."

"Magruder's is having a sale on bacon and it's only 99 cents."

"Wow. That's great."

I inhale his bad breath, which smells of stale cigarette smoke from cheap cigarettes.

I observe how pathetic he is with red lint on his charcoal blazer, knowing that no one will ever pick it off or even tell him it is there. I doubt he will ever know it's there because I doubt he looks in the mirror.

And...

"With bacon 99 cents and lettuce can't be that expensive and I know a Goodwill Hostess where I can get three loaves of bread for the price of one. And when it's on sale I can get five loaves of bread for the price of one..."

And on...

And on...

And on...

He pushes an Altoid around his stale mouth with his tongue while he talks. The mint looks like a loose tooth still connected to his skull by one long nerve ending.

I can't wait to get out of here and drink and smoke and fuck.

I bet the old trout swims home with visions of BLTs for a midnight snack and his only companion resting on his shoulder... red lint on his charcoal blazer.

Moving Through Whores

Sitting in a sterile sports bar, I'm waiting for poetry to walk through that door so we can move to a place with more character and personality.

I sit, waiting, and thinking about how we use doors like whores. We just use them by charging right through them and not caring how we tread or how fast.

And soon, poetry sneaks up slowly behind me sitting at the bar, and throws her arms around me. I can feel her breasts against my back as she hugs me.

I say, "Why don't we move to a bar with more life?"

Poetry takes me by the hand, and moves me right through that easy and willing whore.

Our Skins Steamed Visibly

I fucked her on her living room floor
and came like a champ.

I picked myself up, slowly and naked,
and moved into the bathroom.

I opened the toilet's mouth,
shed my filled condom's skin,
and discarded it into the toilet's mouth.

And then, I chased it with some well-traveled beer.

I moved over to the sink, slowly and naked,
turned on the water,
and began to wash my hands and cock.

Under the running water,
I scratched off the blood that dried
to my right hand's middle finger.

It's always wrong when there's blood involved.
But it's always hotter too.

She's told me before, "Everything feels more
heightened down there, and I feel more wet."

I left the bathroom, slowly and naked,
returned to my lover,
and lay next to her splayed body
naked.

I'm a Little Bit Bitter

Many times
I have sat alone at a table
that has at least two chairs.

I sit in one
and a promise or a possibility
occupies the other.

Too often
that promise or possibility gets stolen away
by a party of people who are too abundant
for the few chairs surrounding their table.

I sit alone and my promise or possibility
is now being sat on by a fat ass.

It always manages to be a fat ass or a lowlife
who steals away my promise, my possibility.

I sit alone
and drink
and smoke

and seethe.

Invalid Theology

Everybody's a comedian.

And if not,
they have religion.

Everybody has an opinion.

And those with really bad ones
manage to be the most vocal.

And many times the most opinionated vocal ones
are bad comedians,

but they manage to find a stage or a platform
somewhere.

And maybe
I should just
shut up.

Tending Bar

I enjoy seeing people filled with passion, especially if it's angry. Like Pat the Bartender when three drunks joked about paying their tab. I had never seen Pat so stern, but he was stirred by an angry passion.

"No, seriously fellas, you have to either pay with cash or pay with a credit card."

One of the three drunks fumbled through his wallet with a silly, goofy, toothy smile on his face and his hair was all spiked up and his big bulbous eyeballs were held within large eyelids and he had a big ass goofy fucking tooth teeth tooth teeth toothy smile.

And Pat was filled with such an angry passion that he reached over, grabbed the tooth man's wallet, pulled out some large bills, threw it back at the teeth, and said, "Thanks."

Pat is such a cool motherfucker.

He knows to bring me a beer whenever I walk in and he knows to hand me a pen, medium point Papermate. Well, it's a medium point anyway. He'll soon learn that I write better with Bics.

But I like Pat and I like people who express their angry passion, especially when it means so much to them to get their point across. Even if it is just a medium one.

Bedroom Eyes' Freckles

Bedroom Eyes came up to me today and took me by surprise.

I was facing the opposite direction when she came up from behind me, moved into my view, and asked, "Do you have the time?" while she held her watch, limp in her hand.

And I, startled by Bedroom Eyes before me, collected myself, smiled, looked down at my own watch, and said, "It's 6:30."

And she asked, "Is that the exact time?"

I looked down again and said, "It's 6:32, exactly."

And she moved her bedroom eyes down, rotated the knob around, pulled the watch taut, placed it around her wrist, fastened it, and said, "Thanks."

She then turned and walked away.

And I said, nothing. I was dumbfounded.

But now I smile because I have another detail to add to Bedroom Eyes… Bedroom Eyes has freckles. And they become her very well.

I think, *If I ever see her again, I will tell her that I wrote some poems about her.*

But, when I look back, I realize that what just happened was all I really asked for in the first place: for her to part her lips in passing conversation, and she did.

Thank you, Bedroom Eyes, with your cute freckles and vanilla ice cream lips.

The Grift

I smile because I am a grifter.

I grifted a free beer out of everybody else's tips, and all I did was sit here and allow people to order drinks over me and allow money to pass around me and allow their tips to sit near me and eventually I got a free beer.

And I smile because it's free.

And all the bartender did was ask me if I wanted another and all I did was nod, and they picked up their tips to pay for my beer because they thought that money came from my pocket.

And I smile at my full free beer.

You Know Who I'm Talking About

Please excuse me while I vent.

Fuck these fucking customers who can't appreciate a neatly folded stack of shirts!

I am here for a reason. So don't say, "No, I'm fine," when I ask you if I can help you find your size in that design and then continue rifling through my neatly folded shirt stack. Who is going to know better than me where that fucking shirt is in your size? Not your rifling, destroying hands laying waste to my beautiful stacks. So don't say, "No, I'm okay," because you're not. You don't know what you're looking for and you have no fucking clue where to start, so don't say, "No," you beast of destruction, say, "Yes, I have no fucking clue, please find me this design in a Large. Thanks."

And another thing, no, I will not give you a discount on something that is already on sale. You fuckers are so spoiled that you would still complain if I gave you the merchandise for free and placed a dollar in your pocket. You would still want more. What have you ever done for me? Buy me a coffee. Give me a stick of gum. Slip me a five. Do something for me and I'll consider giving you an additional discount, but otherwise, get over it! I am not lowering the price further, you spoiled bastard.

And one more thing, what the fuck is going on when I find out that I will get a day off, finally, for Easter holiday and I am happy that I can get trashed Saturday night (well, nothing stopped me any other night, but a day off justifies getting trashed even more), and I should be able to sleep in, but then I am informed that I am going to lose an hour because of daylight savings time? What the fuck!??!

But then I realize that everyone who messes up all the shirt stacks and asks for additional discounts all worked retail at one time or another and they are just getting revenge and continuing the cycle of discourtesy and they all have real jobs now and I can't wait to get a real job and fuck up shirt stacks and whine about more discounts and laugh about taking an hour from the retailers on their one day off because it is a big national joke on everyone in retail.

Sorry. I just had to get that off my chest.

One Glorious Coffee with Sugar and Cream

I am looking into the top of my coffee cup.

I am looking at some coffee that reminds me of a toilet I was once disgusted by.

I drink my coffee down anyway.

The Old Trout (III)

The old trout must have some cats because he swims over to me and begins scratching at my bags like a cat.

I say to him, "What the fuck, man?! Do you need a litter box?"

He laughs his gross tooth laugh and says, "No, but I did find myself lapping water out of a glass the other night. I stopped short of putting my bowl of food on the kitchen floor and eating on all fours, but I continue trying to bring my foot up to my ear and scratching."

I reply, "That is a goal I have yet to set for myself."

I think one day I may understand how the old trout's world works, but I hope not.

Transactions

People are strange.

I am pausing in the middle of a transaction while the woman writes a check.

Just then, a pretty woman and her rather fat girlfriend come up to me and ask, "Where's the food court at?"

"There isn't a food court, all the food's spread out. What kind of food are you looking for? What *genre*?" I ask, trying to be funny with my use of the word "genre" and the way I roll it around in my mouth like I was French or something.

They're all business though.

The pretty one says, "We're just looking for something quick, something we can sneak into the movies, like a hot dog or a pizza slice."

I say, "Well, for fast food there's Arby's, Roy Rogers, Burger King…"

"No, no, no. We're just looking for like pizza or a hot dog."

"Sbarro?"

"No, we want a hot dog."

"Okay. How about Frank 'n' Stein?"

And they nod and say, "Yeah."

"Take a right past Everything Yogurt there and it will be on your right."

The pretty woman smiles and I smile back.

I return to the woman writing the check and say, "I could go for a hot dog right now."

She says, "No, they don't sit well with me."

I say, "Yeah, you know, they oftentimes give me headaches."

She asks, "Too many chemicals?"

I say, "Well, at least one too many."

She then recommends that I try kosher hot dogs because they don't put chemicals in their hot dogs, but they do put a lot of garlic.

I say, "Well, I'll have to try those sometime."

I can't believe I just had a discussion about hot dogs with a woman I just sold a green crewneck sweater to.

We are all such a strange breed.

Stirred by a Passion

I was stirred by a passion this evening and my numb mind doesn't know what to make of it.

I surrendered to an evening of leisure after a 12-hour workday, a day that went well. "Well" meaning fast and without incident. I never got stressed. I was never lifted out of my seat and forced to move outdoors. In fact, I never once saw the sun or anything outside.

I went home looking forward to a pizza, a few beers, and a few phone calls and nothing else. But, I was stirred by a passion this evening I had not been prepared for. I called my lover at 11:00 p.m. and found out that she was drunk and that she wasn't alone.

After figuring that out, she said to me through the phone, "I'll call you later," and hung up.

Five seconds later, I was pounding the back of the sofa with my fist and throwing my shoes back and forth across the room and pacing. I called again and again and again and she wasn't picking up the phone. Even the answering machine stopped answering and the phone just rang. I began losing my mind.

I jumped in my car and did 100 all the way from my house in Virginia to her apartment in Maryland. I turned a 45-minute drive into 20. On the radio, as if on cue, the band Body Count raged *"There goes the neighborhood..."* And there was nothing on my mind but an excuse for a cop and a homicide or two.

Once I arrived, I called somebody else in the building and made up a story that admitted me through the front door. I raced up four flights of stairs and stood before Apartment 419 and began pounding on the door.

"Oh shit," I heard her say. "I can't believe it." This was followed by a commotion of shuffling.

"Open this fucking door!"

And there was shuffling – and shuffling – and, "Oh shit" – and mumbling. Mumble, mumble.

I just kept pounding.

She eventually stepped through the door, out of the darkness and into the light of the hallway.

And me, "What the fuck are you doing?"

"I'm drunk."

"Yeah? No shit!"

She was standing there with a lit cigarette in her hand and she shrugged at me and said, "What? What?"

I knocked the cigarette out of her hand and the force of the blow knocked the cherry from the stem and it sat there, one dead cigarette.

She tried talking me down, "I want a ring. I want to marry you. I love you so much. Don't you love me?"

I said, "Well, I'm here aren't I?" And to me that seemed enough.

She eventually got me to leave when she assured me that there was nothing going on and he was not staying the night.

I picked up the dead cigarette and moved down the hall with the dead cigarette between my lips unlit. I paused between the second and third floor and took a piss in the stairwell's corner.

I returned to my car and began to drive away, but thoughts continued nagging me and I started hearing my best friend in my head yelling at me for not storming in and kicking that guy's ass.

I did a quick U-turn and sped back and tried to phone her first, but it just rang and rang and rang. And my mind thought and thought and thought the worst, of course.

I called another sucker to buzz me in and went back to pounding Apartment 419's door. I heard movement between the living room and the bedroom and then she busted through the door saying, "Fuck! What? I just want to sleep!"

And me, "I thought he was leaving? What the fuck is he still doing here?"

She tried to assure me that nothing was going on, that she loved me, that she wanted to marry me. I just wanted to kick that guy's ass because my best friend was screaming at me in my mind.

I told her, "I can't leave."

She said, "I love you. I know we have a future. This means nothing. Don't you love me?"

"Well, I'm here again, aren't I?" And it still seemed enough, but it wasn't.

She said, "I want you to be my husband."

I said, "Why?" But then I said, "I want you to be my wife." And, "I love you too."

She said, "This means nothing," as she nodded back behind her.

I wondered why she was whispering this fact to me.

"Okay," I said.

Now, I guess I am engaged, but I don't know.

I wish I had more guidance. I wish I were more violent. I wish I were more drunk. I wish I were more simple. And I wish I were more sure, but I don't know.

I guess I'm in love, because I was stirred by a passion that moved me to action, but I just don't know if she's the one. Or maybe there isn't a one, just a two that exists. I wish I knew what love is so I could identify it and squeeze it tight.

I moved down the hall once again and was assured that the guy was sleeping on the couch. I never saw him, but he was either a limp dick wuss or a big fucking linebacker or maybe he didn't even exist at all.

And maybe none of this happened.

And maybe I really am in love.

And maybe I really am engaged right this very minute.

BLANK BOOK FIVE

April – May

Siren Trouble

Earlier tonight, I caught up with a young girl I hadn't seen in a while.

She once came to me for a job, but I didn't hire her because I thought she was so beautiful and I sensed trouble. I knew that I would want more than just work from her, so I did us both a favor. I figured it was better to let her go and lose her among the rest.

She found another job in the same building, so I would still see her from time to time. There was something else there than just her beauty. Something potent and creative was simmering underneath. I could see it in her movement. She was a deadly bottled potion, waiting to be spilled out.

I moved to another building and time continued to pass.

I didn't see her again until she bumped into me tonight. It had been a while, but we recognized each other, stopped, and exchanged pleasantries. How are you? How am I? Glad to see. Etc., etc.

I never asked her what she must have been asked by everyone, "Didn't it hurt to get your nose and eyebrow pierced?" I never asked about her shell, I just stood back and admired her beauty.

But, for some reason, she was very forthcoming about her piercings tonight, without me even asking. She explained how she pierced most of them herself. Anytime she was angry, she would just push a safety pin through her ear and fasten it off.

"Did you pierce your nose by yourself?"

"Yep."

"But not your eyebrow?"

"Nope."

"And not your belly button?"

"Nope. I had those done by somebody else."

And then she revealed, short of showing me, that she had pierced her own nipple. This caused a stir in my pants. She didn't even go into any detail, but I was aroused anyway. I shifted position.

We talked a little bit more and then I left. She gave me her phone number and I made a promise to call. She made a promise to come to one of my readings.

After I left, I felt a twinge. Like there was something left unsaid.

I circled around my car and debated going back in to search for her. I decided, "Fuck it, why not," and went back in. I found her still sitting there.

I said, "Hey."

She said, "Hey." And then she said, "I'm pregnant."

I sat down next to her and said, "Let's talk about it."

And we did. The pregnancy was unplanned.

"I'm sorry. What are you going to do?"

"I don't know."

"How far along?"

"One month."

I stroked her back. I didn't know what else to do.

My Paradigm Shifted

I am trying to figure out the me of before versus the me of now. And I am sorting through how my being has changed, and my thought process has changed, and my love has changed.

My love of another. My love for another.

How is it that I went from not giving a shit to caring a whole hell of a lot? From thinking of only myself to having thoughts that I would do anything for the love of another?

I would cross the path of a bullet. I would throw my chest out at an oncoming train. I would smoke crack cocaine. I would eat shit out of a cow's asshole.

And I would sit here, like I am now, in an empty diner and wait.

A tired waitress sighs expletives under her breath after spilling drinks across the table she just cleaned. She's wishing one big shit upon the world.

And me, alone, finally knowing what love is.

Love is that face that occupies my mind at all times.

Love is looking up every time a door opens and hoping it is her.

Love is having no fear of being alone, just having a fear of being without her.

And love is sitting in this empty diner with only the faintest possibility that she might show up.

I think that is love, but I am still learning. And I hope that I am not too late in realizing.

Kin

A man walks by with strung-out straight blonde hair lying flat across his forehead and down the sides of his head and down the back of his head.

He has wild facial hair cut around his ears, cut around his mouth, cut around his eyes.

He wears a white button-up dress shirt beneath a charcoal wool sweater.

He wears dark blue jeans with the cuffs folded up once, halfway up his shins.

He wears a pair of black Adidas below his folded once blue jeans.

He sips with his facial hair surrounded mouth from a coffee made in Nordstrom's.

I am watching fashion create itself and see the fashion to be worn by people sometime next year.

Curse my fucking pen for bleeding all over this page!

The man with the straight blonde hair and crazy facial hair throws his hand up in the air and talks out loud to no one but himself.

Purgative

"The more you force yourself, the more you won't get it."

This was advice from a friend as I struggled to remember an idea I had just a few hours before and, *Fuck*, if I couldn't remember what it was.

It wasn't just an idea, it was a connection of ideas ready to be placed on the page. A connection of ideas that made sense because they made no sense at all.

Actually, there really was no connection, just a succession of ideas that seemed to go together. That *seemed* to *go* together.

Now this feels like I'm forcing it and I'm still not getting it and, *Fuck*, I know it would have been good.

I'm slipping.
I'm stumbling.

I'm struggling to remember what I once had together, but now, it's gone.

I'm blank.

I'm losing it. I know that if I don't find myself led to the madhouse, there is a possibility that I will regress back to childhood in my old age. It's a possibility that rests in my genes and there's nothing I can do about it. But, with those same genes and the possibility of childhood in my old age, I am secure in the certainty of having a full head of hair while doing it. I may go crazy or be reduced to a diaper, but I will still be cool with a full head of hair. Being both insane and bald would sure suck.

But still… blank.

I give up and throw my bleeding pen aside to allow the wounds to dry and heal.

In disgust, I move to the bathroom to take a piss. The urinal is occupied so I move into the stall and look at a toilet someone forgot to flush.

During the course of my piss, while looking at someone else's shit, my succession of ideas comes back to me.

Now, I am suddenly happy.

I move back to my still bleeding pen and squeeze glorious pain all over the page. I smile, relieved.

Richard

Now, it's not just the old trout I have to figure out, there's a new guy, Richard.

He walks in and seems to have a friendly enough demeanor and I ask him how he is doing and he replies, "Oh, all right, I guess." And that's about it for conversation with Richard.

I observe, and others I know observe, and we try to figure out why he doesn't eat and why he doesn't drink and why he doesn't go to the bathroom. He doesn't do any of these. Not once during an entire seven-hour shift. He just stands there.

But, he does burst out into spontaneous laughter for no apparent reason. And he smiles. A lot.

He seems harmless.

We watch him like we watch others, because what else can you do when you work in a mall but pick apart people and discuss their odd behavior?

Like now... I watch an elegant woman in a flower dress move into my view from the left and I see her move her hand back to her ass and start picking at it. I laugh quietly to myself as this act is exaggerated in my mind and I imagine her hand getting sucked up her ass.

She moves across my view, my eyes passing from her and arriving at Richard. He hasn't moved from his spot.

Come to think of it, I have never even seen him sit down, even though he has a chair to sit in. He doesn't eat, he doesn't drink, he doesn't use the bathroom, and he doesn't sit.

But, wait. What's this?

We observe him move away from his spot and we revel in his motion as he moves to the trash can and throws something away. This action is triumphant to us because it signifies that he actually has a heartbeat. We always suspected, and now it's confirmed.

He moves right back to his spot and stands there, smiling.

My fellow observer leans over and says, "I think he has something in his mouth."

I say, "Yeah, I think he has teeth."

We laugh. A little too loudly, I guess, because Richard ducks from our assaulting laughter and, seeing his ducking motion, we quiet our laughter to giggling so as not to further upset Richard's fragile equilibrium.

Nothing goes unnoticed by a pair of working mall eyes, especially when boredom and time look for anything. Something, anything. An elegant woman picking at her elegant ass. Or Richard finally moving and doing something, if only just to throw something in the trash.

Of All the Shit That Has Happened to Me

I get into my car after a 12-hour workday and think about how the only time I feel secure is when I am in my car, driving away. Then I think, *Even that will likely change soon.*

And, sure enough.

I am on the on-ramp and there is construction along the right shoulder which is protected by a long wall of waist-high concrete pilings. As a result, the merge onto the highway is a lot shorter than it would normally be. Plus, this on-ramp merges with another on-ramp which then merges onto the highway.

I look to the left at the parallel on-ramp and see a car I am about to clear. My mind calculates that I will easily pass him if I accelerate a little, so I press on the gas. And when my eyes adjust back forward, while simultaneously accelerating, I see... *Brake lights?*

"Shit!!!"

My body reacts like one giant nerve. I slam on my brakes, the car slides, and I connect with the brake lights in front of me. And then the car behind me slams into me too and my right arm shoots up to protect my face and BANG! my air bag explodes and dusty smoke fills my car and I inhale and I cough as my car comes to a stop after rolling forward a short distance.

I put the car in park and open my windows.

I step out of my car, slam the door shut, and yell, "Fuck!"

I move over to the concrete pilings and lean with my arms folded across my chest and feel that now, now everything is complete, everything makes sense. Dusty air bag smoke rises out of my car windows and I wait.

I wait for a cop.
I wait for death.
I wait.

Time passes.
A couple cops show up.
And a fire truck.

Once it's all said and done, the person I hit was braking because of some idiot woman in front of him who panicked when she saw the concrete pilings ending in front of her and she didn't think she was going to clear the car that even I had calculated that I was going to clear, so, instead of accelerating, she decided to slam on her brakes.

The guy that I hit tried to claim that I knocked his car into hers, but I was not able to confirm that. All I could tell, with any certainty, was that I hit him and I got hit.

I explain everything from my point of view to the cop. Whether he hit her before I hit him, or I caused him to hit her, I honestly could not say. I didn't understand the ramifications of anything I was saying, I just spoke the truth as I knew it.

I could see, though, that the idiot woman that he hit was

going to be a problem.

She started complaining about her neck and put on a nice show. Because the guy that I hit had hit her, it was starting to look like he was going to be in some kind of trouble by the way she was carrying on and pointing her finger, which I thought was shit, since this lady was an idiot and a fake.

Insurance information is exchanged. The cop writes me a ticket for "not paying full attention," which I think is kind of funny. Who knew that "not paying full attention" is a ticketable offense? I will have to go to court and declare to a judge "guilty" or "not guilty" for the offense of not paying full attention.

I go to work the next day and my world feels fully crushed. The one place I felt safe in was my car, and now even that has been ruined.

A stupid person comes up behind me and pokes me in the back.

I turn and say, "Don't touch me."

She keeps poking me. I whip around and give her a lethal look. She leaves me alone.

Later, she asks me if I want to fill out an application for a department store credit card.

I think, *Give me a break. Please think for me, because I can't bear to. I have put my signature to enough shit over the past couple of months to know better.*

I say, "No, thanks."

Just last week, I was shaking and poring over the rules and regulations just to get a damn membership at the local video club so I could rent the movie *Barfly*.

"Do you hate people?"

"No, but I seem to feel better when they're not around."

My thoughts exactly.

Royal Blue Scuffed Upon Navy Blue

I noticed some royal blue paint scuffed on her navy blue high heels and I wondered how that happened. But, I didn't ask, I was too distracted by her fine ass.

"Alcohol on my hands/ I got plans"

"But I got a drug and I got the bug/ And I got something better than love"

Now, I'm writing at the bar with a cigarette in my hand and a Rolling Rock in front of me and Andy's tending. He has worked behind this bar for a long time and he serves me like an old and tired friend and lights my cigarette like any practiced bartender should, and he answers the phone with utmost sincerity.

"Thank you for calling Hell, this is Andy, how may I help you?"

Hell's my favorite bar in the D.C. area and Andy's my favorite bartender ever. Tonight, Andy's cursing the death of Kurt Cobain, but he's glad that bastard is dead.

"I'm glad that guy's finally worm food."

I don't think he means it. I think he's either trying to be controversial or funny, I haven't figured out which.

My mind wanders back to the royal and navy high heels whose owner's ass I just busted, because that ass is so fine. We went to Annapolis and I highly recommend hooking up with a chick who recently acquired a corporate-approved American Express card because that ass will buy you a Jacuzzi suite for the weekend and fuck you until you're bone dry.

And I'm fucked-up drunk now, but I'm in love, because me and that fine ass were gone for a weekend and we were back in her apartment for no more than 15 minutes when two different guys who want to fuck her called her which indicated to me that they have probably been trying to reach her every hour, on the hour, since we've been gone.

And I smile. Because I love her and she loves me.

I suck on my Rolling Rock and suck on my cigarette and smile. She's probably calling those two nice guys back now and I can't believe she was actually considering settling on a nice guy when she knows that she will never have a cock better than mine.

Fucked-Up Love

I love her...

and I think she loves me...

and I love her and...

FUCK – I'm drunk...

and FUCK – I'm fucked up...

and FUCK – I love her...

and FUCK – I think she loves me...

and FUCK – I DON'T KNOW...

but FUCK – it feels right...

and FUCK – I know it's right...

FUCK – I love her...

I hope she loves me.

I Got This Gift

It all comes around to me.

And while placing my carefully picked grocery items on the belt, I notice that I seem to be partial to grocery items colored yellow, orange, and red.

Egg Bagels
Home Pride Bread
Nacho Cheese Doritos
Single-Size Celeste Pizza
Safeway Cola
Carl Buddig Ham
Bud Light

All yellow, orange, and red like a fire marching slowly down the beltway.

This makes me think, *I wish I would start seeing the smoke before the fire.*

Because I owe the IRS 1,000 dollars and I owe the state of Maryland 600 dollars and I owe GEICO 240 dollars and I owe my car 1,800 dollars (well, 250 dollars deductible anyway) and just to put life into the recently deployed air bag alone will cost 600 dollars.

I am dazed by the fire but am shaken from my thoughts because I now owe the lady 28 dollars and 39 cents for placing my yellow, orange, and red items into blue plastic bags.

It all makes sense to me as everything marches down the beltway and comes around to this. I only wish that I'd start seeing the smoke before the fire so I can avoid the blues in my future.

I give the woman I owe 28 dollars and 39 cents an even 34 dollars. She takes it and gives me a puzzled look.

I nod at her and think, *Just punch it in there, honey, and see what a four-year college education made me capable of calculating.*

She reluctantly punches it in. And then she understands as she gives me one five and some change.

I pick up my blues and walk away, alone. Just me and my blues. And my ability to calculate change.

Life Shuffles Across the Floorboards

Music is strange.

It fills a room, but it doesn't. I play it loud and it seems to occupy space, but I can't see it, I can only hear it. I look around and nothing moves. Nothing is moved by the music that seems to fill the entire room.

This disturbs me.

I look at a pile of newspapers and nothing – not even a flutter. I look at the videotapes resting on the TV and nothing – just potential, nothing kinetic. I look at the wall and nothing – not even a shadow dancing to the music that seems to fill the room.

This upsets me.

Nothing in this room moves at all. Music continues to play loudly and I contemplate the wasted art creating itself; the unrecorded, uncaptured art creating itself upon a five CD random shuffle CD player.

All seems dead. All seems lost as motion does not exist and art creates itself unrecorded.

I am saddened by the fact that the only motion in this room is me lifting another beer to my mouth and me squeezing more blood from this pen without remorse. My ears are the only testament to the beautiful art creating itself on a random five CD shuffle CD player.

I feel like creating a party of motion in this dead room by opening the windows and allowing the wind to perk everybody up. The newspapers… the photographs on the table… the dead plants in the basket next to the fireplace. But I don't because I don't know what insects might try to crash this party. And…

What's that? What's that slowly moving across the hardwood floors?

I bend down on all fours and look real close.

It's a potato bug moving to the music that seems to fill the room.

With my middle finger, I flick it in the antennae and it curls up into a ball. With that same finger, I send it screaming across the room.

I hate party crashers. Even when any motion is desperately needed. It felt good to flick that prick clear across the room.

I return to my seat and continue admiring the dead stillness and lost art stinking up this whole fucking place.

No Sense of Direction

I wander mentally and I am sick physically.

And I can't eat because of my mental and physical sickness.

I took a wrong turn on a Friday and by the time I realized I was lost, two months had died.

Now, I am sick.

Sick in love, sick about love, sick from love.

And I am puking thoughts.

The pain in my middle does not allow even thoughts of food, much less the passage of actual food. My brain spreads its disease and seems to infect my being, and I'm left weak.

Poetry surrounds me and poetry moves around me and I am left too weak to even lift my pen to put that poetry to paper.

My brain swells with new fears, fears with which I am unaccustomed, because they are fears that I have never crossed paths with before.

I am learning how to cope, and articulate, and handle these fears when they confront me, but it's not easy, and I am weak.

I feel vulnerable, I feel unprotected, stuck in realms I don't understand, like I am bound naked on ice in the open air.

My balls feel cold between my legs against the ice while an entire planet descends on my being bound naked on that ice and all I can do is watch it happen.

I sigh heavily as the disease spreads itself throughout my being.

They are only thoughts, but they are poisonous thoughts, reducing me to a state of debilitation.

Soon, I will be sucking my meals through a straw, as the reality of my cold balls consumes me.

Chip Away

In Retail Hell, each day after day after day, some way after way after way.

One guy I know says, "Hey!" as he rushes by where I'm sitting.

I look up and say, "Hey."

Minutes after this, a girl I know says, "Hey!" as she goes rushing by in another direction.

I look up again and say, "Hey."

Another girl says, "Hey!"

And this time I say, "Fuck! Can't you see I am trying to write? I am writing about you. All of you. All of you that are chipping away at me.

"Didn't you see me writing? And now you've interrupted my train of thought. Could you please back up and do what you just did again? I was trying to capture that moment on paper when you tripped over your own feet and casually looked back, annoyed and confused, but ultimately embarrassed, looking for that misplaced tile that caused you to stumble. To me, that was poetry in motion. Could you do that again, please?

"Fuck. Never mind. The moment is gone now. No, no, forget it, move along. Go on, move along."

She sends me a sideways glance and thinks I'm crazy.

But I think, *Who's the one looking back? You're the one who tripped over your own feet and instead of looking back you should have just looked down at your own two bloody feet.*

It was your deformed and stupid feet that made you trip, not an invisible misplaced tile, so don't look so damn confused. And quit interrupting me when I'm writing.

Thank you.

Something is Pinching

Something is pinching the back of my right eye and there is discomfort. My eyelids twitch trying to ease the pinching, but it's no use, just have to wait the pain out.

I am very happy because I have a very short workday and I feel like a bum breaking every rule in the dress code and not giving one shit about it.

I smile when I think about how I thought I lost my book this morning and searched the entire house attempting to retrace my drunken steps of the night before, but it was no use.

But then I remembered. The night before, I stripped off my clothes and put on some music, and I laid down on my bed with my book in my hands, and I was reading some stuff I recently wrote.

I was reading from my book up above my drunk, pillow-laid head and I can only imagine what happened after that. First, I imagine, my eyes shut. And then my mouth probably relaxed. And then, like a freshly chopped tree, my arms must have fallen to one side, throwing my book between my bed and the wall.

And, sure enough, I found my book between my bed and the wall.

I pulled it out and it opened to a blank page. I looked it over and discovered bite marks all over the blank page and I smiled, because I didn't remember doing it.

And just finding my book between my bed and the wall was enough of a triumph, but to find something new that I did but don't remember was even more satisfying.

Especially when I was probably looking over this blank page, drunken tired, and trying to create something new on this blank page, drunken tired, and the best thing I could come up with was to assault this blank page with my teeth and just bite it.

We

We place so much emphasis on a child's first words and then we're quick to endow them with a vocabulary, so they can better communicate and impress.

We place so much emphasis on a child's ability to read in order to expand their mental capacity, so they can better communicate and impress.

We place so much emphasis on a child's capability to write so they can assemble words on the page with fluidity, so they can better communicate and impress.

And what we grow up to learn (speaking and reading and writing) is that language (spoken or read or written) is limited.

We spend a large fraction of our lives learning that there are vast limitations to our language and to our ability to communicate and impress.

Yet, we try so hard.

We imagine and conceptualize and we soon realize that any attempt at perfect comprehension through communication is in vain.

And yet we try really hard anyway.

I see a child run quickly away from their parent and I'm quietly cheering them on in my mind, *Run! Run! Run!*

I have yet to see one get away, but still I silently cheer them on.

The parent always catches up to them and grabs them and shakes them and pulls them in and carries them back toward routine.

And everything resumes, business as usual. Parents stalking and seizing the only thing that helps them sustain the cycle of absurdity.

I've Had Enough

I am tired.

I can barely keep my arms up, much less continue punching at the invisible opponent who keeps wearing me down. With blows to my middle, and multiple blows to my head, I keep bobbing and weaving, but it's no use. You can't evade an unseen fighter.

At least when you step into a madhouse, you know what you are stepping into. But when you step into a mall, you don't know who's going to come at you and start throwing punches. You just don't know.

A child stands near me and I look in her face as she stands ten feet in front of me and wails. Tears are streaming around her huge screaming mouth. It's a scream that's so shrill you just want to kill.

She wails, tears stream, and she screams after her father who has given up the fight. Her father just abandoned her and left her standing ten feet in front of me.

And then this screaming mouth and streaming eyes feels me looking at her. She turns to me and lowers her shrill to a yell and looks at me angrily.

And all I can think is, *Shut the fuck up, kid. It only gets worse from here.*

She runs to her daddy embarrassed that I have looked upon her screaming and streaming.

I have had enough.

I am tired.

Get me out of this fucking place.

Please, place me before an opponent I can see. Or please, knock me out and put me out of my misery.

Dave (Fake Fucking Bastard)

I was just sitting here at work minding my own business on a Thursday. I was thinking about a beer at a bar anywhere. Anywhere but here.

I feel a pair of eyes on me and look up to see the cover of GQ passing in front of me, staring at me real hard.

I look at his slick-backed hair and his well-tailored suit and his little shoes with the tassels loose on top and he is eyeballing me as he passes in front of me.

He passes by and makes a big U-turn as he begins to circle back, suddenly remembering me.

And I am still sitting here minding my own business.

He speaks, "Weren't you the dude who read in that place in Adams Morgan this past Sunday night?"

"Probably."

"Yeah, your stuff is cool."

"Thanks."

"Don't you remember me?"

"No."

"I was the dude that was there wearing the tie-dye shirt and the black leather biker jacket and a black do-rag on my head and torn blue jeans and I read my poem about riding my motorcycle on the West Coast and stuff."

"Sounds familiar." *Probably because it sounds like every fucking cliché associated with poetry writers and Beat wannabes.*

"Yeah, I don't like to dress like this at night, I just like to let loose."

I look down at myself, suddenly conscious of the fact that I have been wearing the same clothes ever since that reading four nights ago. I am overwhelmed by a desire to bathe and comb my hair. And then I think, *What am I thinking? Who gives a shit! At least I feel comfortable in my skin. This bastard leads a fake existence by day and a fake existence by night.*

"Hey, man, I'm a little busy here. Can't you see I'm busy?" Actually, there's really nothing going on and I don't have anything else to do.

"Dude, I was just talking to you. I'm new in town and I plan to go back to that place in Adams Morgan all the time."

I think to myself, *Great, now this fuck thinks we're friends.*

He continues to talk to me about his fake job through his fake smile and I can't stop looking at the greasy little helmet of hair on his head and I can't stop looking at his little shoes with his little patterned socks and, *Fuck, shut up! Leave me alone!* I want to yell this, but I don't.

Eventually, he shakes my hand and moves away.

"Welp, I gotta go to lunch, dude. See you on Sunday."

"Great, I can't wait."

He moves away from me with his back straight, and sometimes it's just so easy to hate.

Sunday arrived. I think I changed my clothes. I know I bathed at some point (or it rained).

And I can't seem to lose that cloud that is hovering over me, perpetually dumping on my head. I almost managed to ditch it while speeding in my car on the highway, but, as soon as I stopped, it caught up with me and dumped large raindrops on my windshield, awakening me to more reality.

Fortunately though, there was no black leather clad tie-dye in sight that Sunday night.

But, just when you think you've lost the storm, it manages to find you somehow…

I go to an old familiar coffeehouse that I haven't been to in a month and it seems clean, or maybe, it seems clean in relation to me.

I sit myself down at the bar and I realize that I enjoy moving from bar to bar, whether it's for coffee or for beer. I enjoy the overall aesthetic.

I sit down next to my friend Bert and we talk and

drink unidentifiable things. Hot things in tan and black delivered in cracked mugs and we manage to laugh and smoke cigarettes while doing it.

Then, in through the front door saunters a black do-rag atop a black leather biker jacket.

All I can say is, "Oh shit."

And over towards me, remembering me, drifts my black full fat fucking cloud.

"What's wrong?" asks Bert.

I whisper back, "You'll see."

My cloud pulls a stool up next to me and says, "Hey dude, how's it goin'?"

"Oh, hey." I act like I just noticed him.

He removes his black leather biker jacket and displays a turquoise long-sleeve turtleneck beneath a partially buttoned turquoise pin-stripe dress shirt with the sleeves rolled up the arms to reveal an expensive watch attached to the outside of one of his long-sleeve turquoise turtleneck shirt sleeves and, *Ugh! The pain! Somebody please shoot me.*

He turns away from me and asks Heather for a Coke with ice.

I laugh.

Heather says, "We don't have Coke here."

He shifts and says, "Can I have a coffee then?"

Heather begins to move away, but he adds, "And can you put ice in that?"

She turns back slowly and says, "Sure."

Oh, the pain... the pain....

Fortunately, my cloud floats over to the corner and leaves me.

I watch as he places all of his stuff down, and places all of his stuff in a particular order that he must have organized in his mind, now transferred onto the table in front of him.

He sits back and sips his iced coffee.

I look away. It's too painful.

I look to my right and on the bar sits a marble-colored calligraphy pen which must have cost a fortune and couldn't belong to anyone but my cloud.

I pick it up and bring it over to him.

"Hey, is this your pen?" as if I don't already know the answer.

"Hey, yeah. Thanks, dude. Now I can write."

I cringe at this, but say, "That's a nice pen. If that were my pen I would report it to my insurance."

"Yeah, dude, I can't write without it."

"Uh huh." *You can't write with it either. Dude.*

I return to the bar and pass an occasional glance in my cloud's direction, hoping to forecast the next storm.

I watch him as he stabs the page with his expensive pen. It is a gruesome sight.

Write a sentence.
Lay the pen down.
Grab up the iced coffee.
Lean back.
Ogle women.
Sip.
Ogle women.
Sip.
Think.

Look down at the dying, mutilated page.

Think.
Lean forward.
Put iced coffee down.
Pick up the pen.

Stab, stab, stab more wounds into the page.
Set the pen down.
Pick up the iced coffee.
Lean. Look.

Think. Sip.
Look. Sip.
Think.

Iced coffee down.
Pen up.
Stab. Stab.

Pen down.
Iced coffee up.
Lean, look, sip.
Look, think.
Look, sip.
Look, think.
Look, look. Look, look.
Sip, think.

Iced coffee down. Pen up. Stab, stab, stab.

I squeeze my eyes closed. It's too much pain. I can't stand it.

Sometimes, it's just so easy to hate.

I keep sucking away at my tan and black and continue to outrun my clouds, sometimes.

And that poor page lays flayed on the table while my storm leans back, sips, and thinks about raining more blows on that paper.

A Song and Dance Routine

She was one of the most horrible dancers I had ever seen. She was one of the most horrible dancers *anyone* had ever seen.

I stood behind her and watched her struggle to perform for the audience. She couldn't seem to find the rhythm. She moved around to music that no one else could hear but her.

But, she is my Italian wet dream…

She moved awkwardly before me, but I couldn't stop thinking about her as the girl I once knew and it made her dancing sexy to me. She finished her dance and backed out facing the crowd and she backed right into me and she backed right into my erection.

"Oooooh! Well, hello there. What's this?" she giggled with her large sexy toffee eyes as she reached behind and grabbed at my erection through my pants.

Her motion backing into me caused me to throw my arms around her body and I embraced her from behind.

I whispered in her ear, "Why don't we move outside?"

She said, "I am not the figure of youth that I used to be. I'm feeling kind of fat."

I said, "Baby, you are fat in all the right places. That's why I find you so fucking lusty."

"Oooooo," she purred. "Let's go."

We moved outside and onto some grass between the intersection of two sidewalks. It was the middle of the day and the sun was bright. There were high rises everywhere and I just knew that people were watching us. We found a smooth section of grass.

I scooped up her large breasts from behind by passing my hands underneath her arms and grabbing hold. Her large breasts felt good outside her tight sweater. I turned her around and removed her tight sweater, and then I helped her remove her tight pants.

She peeled away all of my clothes until there was nothing left except my erection.

Soon, we were facing each other on the smooth grass naked, feeling taut with anticipation.

My Italian wet dream was so sexy.

She threw me down and the smooth grass blades felt good against my back. She threw one leg over my middle and this action spread her wet pussy open to my cock. She slid her wet pussy slowly down onto it. And, *Oh*, that felt so fucking good. She started riding me, up and down, up and down. I enjoyed watching her large breasts move up and down, up and down, and around until I caught them with my hands and squeezed them tight. I joined her in the motion, now that I had a firm hold. *FUCK, FUCK, FUCK*, that felt good.

She had no problem finding the rhythm to that song.

She opened her mouth then and closed her eyes and started singing. She not only had the rhythm, she also knew the words.

With her head thrown back and her eyes closed and her mouth open, she began singing her song. She continued to dance her dance to her song, and I was loving this fucking show.

The band was moving. The band was moving. The band was building up to something dramatic. Soon, she let out a long, high-pitched conclusion. Her conclusion slid down all sides of my cock.

And then, silence.

It was my turn to conduct. I tossed her off of me and onto her back.

"Oooooh, ewwwww," she squealed with pleasure.

I was soon upon her.

I spread her legs and looked down at her glistening full lips. I looked at each breast as they hung slightly to both sides of her. I collected them up in my hands and thrust my erection into those full wet lips and pumped out an inspired little ditty. My hands moved with each breast's beat as I pumped faster and faster and faster and then I threw my head up high in the air, gritted my teeth, squeezed my eyes, and paused there for a moment until my ditty sputtered out and ended.

I then collapsed on top of my Italian wet dream.

We received some strange applause from a passing cloud that decided to pause and look down at our musical dancing show.

Soon, applause could also be heard coming down from the high rises which had just witnessed the greatest song and dance of all.

I awoke from my full-breasted Italian wet dream and was disappointed when, once again, there was no product of that amazing dream in my sheets. *Damn!*

Someday, someday. That was just too fucking intense. Someday, I will make those sheets very sticky, and I will finally be able to proclaim that I have had at least one wet dream in my lifetime.

Then I can check that one off my list.

Collisional Gravity and a Court Date

1.
"Things happen for a reason."

No.

"That happened because God willed it to happen. God has a proper order of events that are all predestined."

No, shut up.

"It was your destiny that it happened, there was nothing you could do to prevent it."

No, that doesn't work either.

It is so alluring to accept simple explanations for why bad things happen. It allows the human mind to keep from dwelling on traumatic moments for too long.

There must be some kind of equation that allows you to plug in all the factors and all the variables and all the components and arrive at a satisfactory conclusion.

Instead of attempting to justify the ends, why don't we focus on the means that resulted in those ends?

How about this: "Collisional Gravity."

That sounds good. It doesn't mean that you are predestined towards a moment or a traumatic event. It means that you are forced or pulled into them.

I did not crash my car into that other car because it was predestined by God in some grand scheme of things. It was Collisional Gravity. My car was pulled into that other car by an unseen force of gravity.

So, Judge, I submit that the fault is not mine, nor my car's, for colliding into the back of his car. But rather, it was his car that sucked us into a collision, and it is his car that should be punished. A grievous act of Collisional Gravity caused my car to be involved in that accident. I was merely an observer, my car just a pawn, in this whole ordeal. His car is the only guilty party here.

I rest my case, your Honor. Thank you.

I practiced this theory and this speech in my mind as a joke and obsessed over my impending court date, as if what I was charged with was going to need to be defended somehow. I had no idea what I was in for and it was making me nervous.

Plus, there's something about admitting your guilt that instinctively makes you want to fight against it, no matter how paltry the charge is. It seems against our nature to actually utter aloud the words, "I'm guilty."

2.
My court date arrived. My appearance in the courtroom was brief.

The judge asked, "Mr. Gerding, is it?"

I replied, "Yes, sir."

"The officer has charged you with, it says here, 'not paying full attention.' How do you plead?"

"Guilty, your Honor."

"Very well. Please pay the fine before you leave the courthouse today."

And that was it.

Up next was that idiot woman who caused all of this to begin with and she was prepared to put on quite a show. She looked completely rehearsed and had a lot of props. She even wore a neck brace.

I passed the guy that I hit and he looked concerned. That idiot woman was clearly going to drag this out and she was going to drag him with her. The longer she delayed her share of the responsibility, the longer it delayed the processing of his insurance. And, of course, she had no insurance of her own. Hence, the theatrics.

As I left the courtroom, I heard the judge ask her, "How do you plead?" And she said, "Not guilty, your Honor," very defiantly. And then she started to say more, but the judge cut her off by telling her to, "Save it," and set a future trial date so she'd have an opportunity to state her case then.

I didn't care. It didn't affect me. I was guilty and I was done.

BLANK BOOK SIX

May – August

Just One Big Mouth, Please

He asked me, "Is scruffy facial hair in?"

"What?"

"Is scruffy facial hair in?"

"Don't ask me what's in, or even what's been. I don't know. Why are you asking me?"

"Because I noticed you were wearing a couple days growth."

"What are you taking notes? I haven't had time to shave. So what? Leave me alone."

I feel like I've wasted a lifetime if it takes me longer to decide what to wear than it takes me to blink.

And don't ask me what I was doing that Tuesday last month because I can barely remember the events of this past Tuesday (which was yesterday).

Come to think of it, I am still trying to remember what was disturbing me just earlier today.

Oh yeah, now I remember...

I passed a man earlier today who looked like he had the weight of AIDS resting on his eyelids and Iron Maiden was molding his earlobes gray.

Then, a moment later, I was disturbed by a woman I was passing (or, more like, avoiding) whose arms were flailing wildly around her like runaway garden hoses as she was speed-walking by in unpredictable directions.

I quickly returned to my seat as if it were "base" and I was caught in some life-threatening game of "tag."

And now, I sit and slump under the weight of humanity.

And now, I sit and slump under the weight of insanity.

And now, I sit and slump under the weight of the demands of the fashion industry.

Please leave me alone, I don't know.

I crumple in my seat like a partially crushed beer can and wait for the inevitable end.

My eyes follow a mother with a babe in her arms and I watch as the mother points and asks her daughter, "See the frogs? See the frogs? See the frogs? You want me to get you a T-shirt with frogs on it?"

"NO! Me want a Mickey's!" The girl crosses her arms in defiance and pouts.

Half of my mouth creeps up into a grin and, *Yeah kid, I hear you. Me want a Mickey's too.*

Mike and Dike
(A Poem in Two Acts)

Act One: *One Friday Night*

I arrive at the clean, well-lighted sports bar and pull up a stool next to my girl and her girlfriend.

I deliver my line to the bartender (which I was practicing before my arrival) like a jittery young thespian on opening night who is suddenly illuminated by the spotlight.

"Whichever light beer is the cheapest beer is the beer that I want a pitcher of now!"

"No problem."

Relief rushes over me as the anxiety of delivering the first line is past me. I can now concentrate on the unraveling of this silly production.

The bartender moves quickly back and forth in his cage. He fills up a pitcher and he grabs up a pint glass and he slides both across the bar towards me. The pitcher slides to a perfect stop in front of me, but his miscalculation of the lighter more fleeting glass causes it to slide right past me and onto the floor.

Needless to say, no miracle was going to save that glass from death. And what a glorious death it was, as it exploded into several pieces all over the floor. That scene in the play successful, I deliver my next line.

"I didn't ask for a glass anyway, I only asked for a pitcher!"

I throw my hands around the pitcher and I slap my big silly lips on the pitcher and I drink directly from the pitcher as if this had never been done before.

My girl and her girlfriend continue to talk with each other as I look around and take in the set which is of a clean, well-lighted sports bar. I am suddenly disgusted by the order of the set and the cleanliness of the set. It bothers me. It has no character.

I feel as though I have stepped into a fresco by Michelangelo. A collection of well-chiseled perfect human beings and a sprinkling of pixies and putti here and there to keep the perfection well-balanced.

It makes me sick.

I move into the bathroom and cleanliness and order lurk even there. I decide to piss all over the floor and I scale the urinal to displace a ceiling tile and two. I feel much better having done this.

Michelangelo would have been really pissed, as I picture him replacing the ceiling tiles and mopping up my urine with paper towels while grumbling expletives, "Fuck this, fucking shit!" You know, but with an Italian accent.

I move back to the bar, satisfied.

But, I am quickly angered again when I discover that a pixie and her fat putto friend are conspiring to snake some of my beer from my pitcher. They have constructed a pipeline of straws and are attempting to use it as a siphon.

"Bastards! Blasphemes!" As I chop down their pipeline with my hand. "No! Back off! Away with you, you evil, evil politicians! Trying to suck my beer into revolution. I will have none of it! Status quo! My beer stays here! Bastards!"

It seems my tirade has vanquished the pixie and her fat putto friend because when I turn around again, they are gone.

I soon grow tired. I grab my girl and we move away from the clean, well-lighted sports bar.

We start having sex on the stage, in the spotlight, before the capacity crowd.

It was improvised and totally inspired by the moment. The scene only called for some light lovemaking, but we turned it into something more hardcore.

The act ends. Intermission begins. The audience rises from their seats and erupts into applause. I guess they appreciated our impromptu interpretation of the script.

Intermission ends.

Act Two: *One Sunday Night after One Friday Night*

I enter stage right with only one nickel in my pocket and a backpack on my back.

I make the homeless man angry by apologizing to him and explaining to him that I have no money.

He sees through my deception and knows I have a nickel. He sneers at me and spits at me and turns his back in disgust and shuffles away.

I shrug and think, *Whatever. He's crazy if he thinks I am going to hand over my one and only nickel, especially when I know these five cents have magic.*

I pull my backpack closer and descend the stairs into Hell.

Hell has a bartender. His name is Andy.

There are two women here tonight, which is two more people, regardless of gender, than I have ever seen in Hell before on a Sunday night. I am used to entering Hell and just exchanging lines with Andy and no one else.

But tonight, it's different.

One of them is learning how to ballroom dance while Andy verbalizes the steps to her from behind the bar.

The other is scraping hot wax from within the votive candles and is shaping the hot wax into little balls and placing them exposed upon the bar.

I pull a stool up close to them, and Andy moves over towards me and asks if I am going to stay. I say that I would like to but I don't have any money.

He says, "Hold on, I think I have something for you."

And from some pit, he pulls out a Mickey's and places that Mickey's in front of me. I thank him, grab it up, and lock lips with that Mickey's big mouth.

I watch the one woman as she continues to ballroom dance, while Andy issues forth his tireless instruction.

The other woman continues scraping hot wax with a melon baller and shapes that hot wax into small balls.

Mickey's keeps shoving its wet tongue down my throat and I welcome it.

If this is Hell, I welcome it.

It is a ritual act of Dionysus being played out by a cast of bacchanals.

What humankind and Michelangelo do not understand is that to embrace Dionysus is to embrace divinity. To embrace Dionysus is to embrace sincerity, not sanctimony.

So dance, dance, dance, and scrape and sculpt hot wax into small balls. Stop running from the serpent and recognize it as your protector and embrace.

Confront your fears, shed your tears, and drink your

beers in homage to everything androgynous.

Erase the divisions, erase the walls, erase the chains, and loosen your tie. It's about time we got in touch with ourselves and removed the barriers between our minds and our bodies. So loosen your tie and get in touch. Get in touch with yourself and abandon being such a tight ass human being.

I drain one Mickey's dry, and Andy hooks me up with a second pulled straight from the pit of Hell and places it directly in front of me. Soon I am locking lips again.

Confront
fears.

Shed
tears.

Drink
beers.

And move. Move, because you feel that you have to.

And do. Do, because you feel that you must.

And move and do, because it is in some god that you must trust. Even if that god is you, blue.

My second Mickey's dies, and Andy, anticipating the abandonment of my soul, finds a nickel laid carefully on the bar.

He smiles, "Maybe next time."

I move up the stairs and out of Hell and I pull my backpack close.

I escape Hell having relinquished my five cents but having hailed triumphant with one small ball of wax clutched deep in my fist. With my free hand, I make a cut in my thigh and place my ball of wax inside. And, just as quickly as I cut my thigh, I close the cut in my thigh, move towards poetry, and wait.

I exit stage right. The curtains close and there is momentary silence as I wait.

I Should Have Been Hauled Away

I go meet my roommate "D" with an excuse to be drinking on a Monday night, as if we need one. There is a championship hockey game on TV. Plus, D has decided he is going to drink his way through the bar's entire book of drinks that are listed in alphabetical order. By the time I arrive, D is already on the letter G and has a drunken determination to reach the letter Z.

D begins ordering me five-alcohol drinks without question and soon I am more wasted than I think myself to be. We are no longer interested in the game on TV; we are more interested in D's game of A to Z.

We also watch as sharks pick at the poor, helpless women seated across the bar from us. There are only two of them – defenseless, vulnerable – versus the endless number of dicks lining up and taking turns. One after another, they swim up and take bites. The women are only two deep. The men are infinite with the persistence of testosterone that runs centuries deep.

Each attempt to pick them up is unsuccessful, but the women are worn down from all the activity as they are reduced to less and less with each passing.

It soon gets late.

The women eventually escape.

I get up from my stool and begin charging through everything real drunk – through space, through doors without effort. I sense each doorframe I move through and feel its weight. I move real fast so as not to be caught. I feel that if I move too slowly through any of the doorframes, I might be trapped by one closing down around me.

I wait outside for D who only made it to the letter P, but that was enough.

He is taking too long.

Fuck it. I get in my car and leave. I tell myself, *We didn't come together anyway, he's got his own car.*

I am flying down the street. My concentration is focused on staying within the lines and on each approaching red light. I finally realize the importance of all those parked cars on the side of the road – it's to protect those nice homes from my drunk driving.

I pull a fast left into our neighborhood. And just when I think I am safe, red and blue bright lights flash in my rearview mirror.

"Shit!"

I am so wasted. I am going to be arrested for sure.

"License and registration," the cop says. After I hand him both, he asks me, "Can you please step out of your car?" Once I'm out, he says, "Place your hands on the car and spread 'em."

"Yes, sir."

He frisks me.

"Okay. Turn around. Where do you live?"

"10115 Farmington."

"Can you recite the alphabet?"

Oh, the irony.

"Sure."

"Well, go ahead."

"A B C D E F G, H I J K L M N O P, Q R S, T T V, W X and Z."

"Is that all?"

"Uh huh."

"Get back in your car."

Oh shit. I am going to be arrested for sure. I am so wasted and I failed the fucking alphabet. I got the rhythm all wrong. In fact, I had no rhythm at all.

At this point, D moves past me in his own car looking wide-eyed and freaked.

I am going to jail. I'm sure of it.

"Can you step out of your car again, please?"

"Sure."

"Walk heel to toe and count out loud up to ten and then turn around and do ten back, heel to toe, out loud."

I manage this task relatively easily and he asks me my address again.

"10115 Farmington."

He tells me to return to my car. He returns my license and registration and tells me to go home.

I can't believe it. I don't hesitate. I just move towards home in disbelief.

I pass D walking towards where I was. I stop and pick him up and he's shocked. He has his checkbook in one hand and his credit card in the other. He thought for sure that he was going to be bailing me out of jail.

I get us home and we both crash to sleep in our respective beds and drunken stupors.

Little is said the next day. We're still in shock that I wasn't arrested.

I tell D that I failed the alphabet and he bursts out into laughter.

"Come on man, that's not funny. I was nearly busted for drunk driving!"

His laughter gets louder and I start to get mad.

I say, "Well, at least I made it to the letter T, you only made it to P."

Okay, This Is Getting Ridiculous

I was in a collision a month ago.

I got stopped, obviously drunk, a week ago.

Now, I am pulled over for blowing through a red light. It's the only traffic signal between where I was and where I was going to and I blew right through it when it was clearly red.

"License and registration."

Familiar with the routine, I grab my license and registration, which are still sitting on the passenger seat from last week's incident, and I hand them to the cop.

"Do you realize what you did?"

"Yes."

"Where do you live?"

"10115 Farmington."

"When do you plan to change your Maryland license to a Virginia license?"

"Soon."

"How long have you lived at 10115?"

"One month."

"Well, take care of your license and be more careful."

"Yes, sir."

He hands me back my stuff and tells me to go.

Unbelievable.

"Thank you, sir."

I don't know how many cops there are here in Fairfax, but I feel like I've received warnings from all of them.

State of Mind

Darkness.
In a crowded room.

Breathing.
The slow inhaling and exhaling of breath heard.

The breathing of many people.

Many people sweating.
A sweat smelled.

A stale smell of many people.

Whispering.
Indiscernible.

More whispering.
In the extreme corners of my skull.

I am trying to hear.

I am trying to hear the unheard.
I am trying to give a voice to the barely perceptible.

But it is difficult to understand.
In the darkness.

The darkness of a crowded room.

And knowing.
Knowing it is crowded.

I yell, "Fuck! Speak up, please! I can barely hear you. Shout it out so I don't miss a word. Scream it. Please, just scream it out loud for me."

Fuck.

Darkness.
In a crowded room.

Salesmen and Flying

"If you don't watch what you say, you might shoot yourself in the foot."

"Flight attendants, please prepare for departure."

I watch, in awe, as the most beautiful pair of breasts moves past in a display of perfection. They are attached to a blonde (but I let this fact fly by, the breasts are much too gorgeous).

"If you don't watch what you say, you might shoot yourself in the foot."

I keep this in mind and allow the perfect breasts to walk by me without saying anything.

A large beer is chasing a Dramamine in my system.

I try to collect my wet imagination that is now spilling all over the floor. This is a difficult process, because so much escapes the limitations of my hands.

"Keep in mind this is a seminar on air filters and understanding the efficiency and arrestance of a number of different media."

You can be sure that my hands are not efficient and are incapable of arresting anyone, much less, capable of restraining my dirty imagination.

The inefficiency of my hands allows the dirt to spread throughout the system, contaminating the entire body and eventually causing a breakdown.

And so goes metaphor after tiresome metaphor....

Like this plane going down the runway. Eventually we're off on some tangent, transcending some plane.

Those gorgeous breasts still go unapproached as my wet imagination soaks into the floor and my hands are no fucking good anyway.

I think about going to the lavatory, stealing another look at perfection along the way, committing it to memory, and putting my hands to better use in self-ecstasy. So pathetic.

Reality to me seems as real as those buildings and intersections down there. Which means, not much.

We move through a cloud and I almost want to puke.

My heart reminds me that it's there.

My mind remembers how high those clouds are when viewed from down there. And now we're passing through them. I push the partition down. One more filter between me and that reality.

I watch as this dumb older lady falters down the aisle before the pilot has indicated it is okay to move about the cabin.

The pilot announces, "We are cruising at an altitude of 60,000 feet."

I did not need to know that.

I purposely drop my gum in the pocket of the seat in front of me.

The pilot announces that this trip is so short, we will not be allowed to move about the cabin.

Shit!

My large beer is knocking on my dick's door, as I frantically toss back pretzels hoping to absorb my large beer, and then realizing how futile that attempt is.

Now, I am frantically tossing back pretzels to empty my pretzel bag so I have something to pee in, in case of an emergency.

The pretzel bag will be an efficient "filter" between my pee and me.

Shit! I got to go. I got to go so bad.

Fuck it, I go.

"Please be careful, sir, the fasten seat belt sign is still on."

The irony will kill me yet as I think about the older lady I was deriding just a moment before.

On the way to the lavatory, I steal a glimpse of the blonde with the beautiful breasts and her posture while sleeping makes her look most unattractive.

She's leaning with her head against the window in such a way that it has slackened her jaw and exposed her large gross teeth. Suddenly, I'm not interested in those breasts so much. In fact, not at all.

I make it to the lavatory and, once inside, I lean my head against the wall to provide me with some balance.

My hips shift around doing the pee-time shuffle, but my head never leaves that wall.

And if the irony doesn't kill me, the fucking turbulence will.

"Flight attendants, please prepare for landing."

The turbulence shakes any last drips from the tip. I snake it back into place and move back to my seat.

I ignore the blonde breasts, not even offering a glance.

The plane turns, and my brain presses down and seems to touch the tops of my eyeballs, and my bowed head thinks about the possibility of a sudden bump snapping my neck down and ending my life.

There is silence as we seem to cruise straight into certain death.

Hopefully the seam will hold strong on this filter and keep contained all the contaminants, thereby keeping the air clean and increasing the efficiency of the system and...

Whoaa!

We hit a rough patch and my leg shoots up in the air and it looks like we might be going for a swim.

Excuse me, you can drop me off here. It looks like I can survive from this height and, yes, I am a very good swimmer.

And then, it's over. It's finally over. We've landed.

As I'm deplaning, the flight attendant says, "We hope to see you again on a future American flight."

"Thank you, no."

Pop! Pop! Down Goes the Enemy
(My Generation)

I slump down into the sofa
becoming one with its coarse texture
as each sharp thread burrows itself
into my skin.

I watch as, one by one, brain cells are slowly being
sucked out of my head and into the television.

A slow passage of death, piece by piece,
as I feel motivation, creativity, and imagination
being leeched from my skull.

And I just watch it happen.

Brain dead and numbed by the products of other brains
tapping into mine and imprisoning mine.

And slowly, brain cell after brain cell
floats away from me.

And I lie there doing nothing. I'm just two eyes with a sofa for a body.

And, *Oh no, not this commercial again...*

"Don't miss the season premiere of a show by the producers of Generation [Puke's] greatest hits, coming in three months."

And I don't move.

And I don't do anything.

My eyes just watch, and my brain cells travel, as I watch another commercial turn a geek into grunge, all on account of being allowed to drive some silly car.

And they claim to be selling the car and not the transformation.

And, *Oh no, not this commercial again...*

"Don't miss the season premiere of a show by the producers of Generation [Puke's] greatest hits, coming in two months."

And my hand scratches at my couch's balls.

And now I'm swatting at the annoying volume of brain cells as they fly more quickly out of my head towards the television and the transference of my brain cells is nearly complete...

"...this Bud's for you, for all you do, the tobacco you chew, the potato stew you poo, this Bud's for you."

And, *Oh no, not this commercial again...*

"Don't miss the season premiere of a show by the producers of Generation [Puke's] greatest hits, coming at the end of the month."

And my finger reaches up and picks my couch's nose.

And the brain cells continue to flow. My skull is almost empty…

"…and detergent really whitens your teeth if you apply it to your vaginal automobile properly. It can also serve as an edible laxative if you have an inflamed colon, but only when you dilute it with the right manufacturer's warning label. This can be done Friday through Sunday between the hours of 8:00 a.m. and 11:00 p.m., but only when directly applying it to the sore area while treating your dog to a light beer and douching with a basketball. All of this must occur during halftime of a beauty pageant for old middle-aged adolescent children under the age of birth. Submerge the strip and properly agitate it for no less than the time it takes an insecticide to kill your neighbor's housekeeper while taking a shower. Then you can properly smile while answering a toaster's cry for help when it doesn't wipe its butt with the right brand of toilet paper and instead brandished a square of sandpaper to remove the zits…"

And, *Oh no, wait. What's this?*

It's the season premiere of that show I don't want to see by the producers of a generation I don't want to be.

And I can't seem to be able to lift my sofa's self up out of its position.

And my eyes remain transfixed on the illuminated cube before me.

And my skull sits empty.

And I watch the season premiere of:
"A Piece of Shit."

Starring:
Some piece of shit.

And I sit,
like a trapped piece of shit.

The Heart Rises to the Throat

My father
follows behind me in a plane.

He watches as my plane
travels not too far out in front of him.

He watches as my plane has one wing clipped
and one-third of the other wing clipped
and soon my plane begins a slow spin.

My father feels this motion in his throat.
It's so real. He's been there before.

He watches as I spin slowly out of reach.
He wants to help but he cannot.
He watches my plane spiral into a dense brush of trees.

The trees look accepting from this height,
as he sees my plane disappear into the trees.

There is no explosion.
There is no flame.
There is no audible crash.

My father circles around and around and around.
The disappearance of me into some forest somewhere.

He soon glimpses me, now an old man,
move out away from that somewhere forest.

I don't look up, I just move away.

Away from the forest.
Away from the experience of my plane's plane.

I am pensive
as I shuffle away from my plane's plane
and move towards some new plane.

My father slowly circles
and watches my movement from above.

Shortly Before Death

The heat is so hot that as soon as I step out of my car, I start sweating. I sweat the sweat of death.

The sun bakes me slowly and is cooking the black pavement beneath my feet white-hot.

The smell of pussy fills my nose, that smell of sweaty female genitalia that sits in a man's mind for days.

I move my slow-roasting self towards the bar looking for relief, but it's too late, my brain is already diseased.

I step through the doorway and no one takes notice and it's not very cool in here either.

I grab a chair and place it on top of an empty table.

Fingers point.
Heads turn.

I pull my hollow hot form up onto the table, collapse in the chair, and wait.

People stare.
Waiting.

I swing one arm up to my chest and pull open my unbuttoned shirt. It falls open and exposes a gunshot wound and two.

People wince and shift in their seats.

But they continue to look. And wait.

I reach up with both hands and shove a finger in each gunshot wound and pinch. People writhe in their seats in discomfort as I move my fingers around and cause the wounds to open further, but they can't look away, they just wince and shift and watch, waiting for whatever's next.

I work the wounds around until there is just one big wound exposing my rib cage and heart.

My diseased brain now cries out for release and commands my hands to release it. One hand holds my head on one side and the other hand closes into a fist and begins beating about the other side. The skull cracks and gray matter is exposed and I start picking at it and throwing it to the ground around me.

My eyes soon close and my body collapses as I tumble forward from the chair, glance off the table, and fall to the ground in one mutilated lump.

People turn back towards their parties.

They continue talking in their dull monotones as if nothing ever happened.

And maybe,

nothing
really
did.

Nature Will Catch Us While We're Sleeping
(if we're not careful)

The sun goes down.

The tide rolls in
attempting to sneak up
on our dreaming.

It moves forward and back
like a drum that is
steadily beaten.

Soon, the tide will beat itself
an unsteady momentum

and envelop us with our
eyes closed and drunk.

Napkin Poem
(Ladies Night)

A cigarette burns out between my fingers
and I am disgusted by that which surrounds me.

I nod for another beer,
but I really just want to leave this place.

It's Ladies Night and there isn't a lady to be seen,
just a lot of early men.

I'm happy because they dispense beer.

The bartender asks for my ID and I frown,
and he looks at my ID, and then he looks at me.

I crack a silly smile and he laughs
and then he gets me a light beer.

A broken defense,
a goal is easily scored.

I spit angered and upset as I become a figure in the
background of someone else's photograph.

This really pisses me off.

The thought of some future beauty
squinting at my face and thinking I'm a cutie.

And the reality of now,
and no one even looking.

Just a twisted face of frustration and disgust
in the corner of a photograph.

The bartender asks for his pen back and I misinterpret
his question because I am deaf and blind.

I say, "Yeah, this pen writes good."

He repeats, "I need to use my pen."

I clutch it to my chest and say, "No, it's mine now."

But, I reluctantly return it because you shouldn't bite
the hand that feeds you.

He uses it and hands it right back.

Napkin Poem
(Current State of Affairs)

Poetry is dying
and I feel alone.

The roots spread easily beneath the sidewalk,
but the tree was barely one foot tall.

Any major branches on display were pruned
well before fruition.

And that was when the sky
began to fall.

I hop from bar to bar waiting for something to happen.

But poetry has never been deader,
and my beer has, at one time, been better.

Napkin Poem
(Diary Entry of a Cigarette on the Day It Dies)

Smoke billows off the end of my cigarette,
like a flag from a pole,

and at the end of its end,
it snaps free its sad soul.

I watch as that soul flies off to one side
and then to the other

and it surrounds me
as I sniff in its whole.

It looks solid as it floats there momentarily,
but then it changes direction and shifts shape.

It slaps me in the face,
then collapses around my space.

I see death
as I stab at its life with my pen
and inhale its sad soul.

I brush ashes from the napkin
on which I write.

I'm sad.

The cigarette shows no remorse
as it burns the poetry I am writing.

Its fiery cherry attempts to destroy
the diary of its existence.

I suck at the cigarette for furtherance
of my own pathetic resistance.

Because that's all that life is,
a pathetic resistance of death.

Why not give up and allow that flag
to snap your soul free,

and be… something.
Something else.

Anything else.

Napkin Poem
(Doggy Style on Texas-Hot Nights)

I don't know where to deposit my seed for further advancement.

I lift the pint glass to my face so I can drain the last of my beer, but instead I knock the rim of the glass into my teeth. If I weren't so drunk, I might have cared.

A clove cigarette seduces me while I ponder how it is that I might die.

I don't know what is easier: a fat ass, a fat beer, or a fat cigarette sucked deep into my hollow center.

Old people surround me as I sit at one corner of the bar.

I don't know what to do as my borrowed pen streaks across this napkin, borrowed from a fat ass belonging to a beauty.

All I can think about on these Texas-hot nights is sex doggy style, laying it into a large ass.

The old people think I am scrawling on this napkin a letter to my mom asking for some money, but I am really writing about them.

They buy me beers anyway.

Dry Fucked Twice

I got a lover and she shows me how to understand the hand as part of the plan.

She arches her back while riding my cock, her tits looking serious as they reach up towards the ceiling.

It wasn't but twenty minutes ago that we had a good laugh when she managed to miss the bed by a good foot – foot and a half.

She was simply an elegant shadow, working her way over, and when she put a knee up and an arm out, her shadow quickly fell straight past the bed and landed somewhere on the ground.

And then, laughter. Laughter that seemed to stretch on forever.

And then, we made love. Even though she said she was scared of me.

"You scare me."

"Why? I'm harmless."

"I don't know, you scare me."

"You're the one on top."

"But, you scare me."

"Whatever, just keep teasing my cock."

And soon, sleep.

Throughout the world I hear men weep.

But, I am not concerned. And I am definitely nothing to be scared of.

I don't think.

Tripping in a Grocery Store

A man is hanging by his tie, dead.

All the food is being incarcerated. The vegetables and fruit need to be released, need to be freed.

A homeless man wearing green is hostilely engaging an unseen enemy. He throws his arms about him violently, then tackles his invisible foe to the ground, and seemingly defeats him.

He gets up and moves on to his next opponent.

Johnny got his gun
and Memorial Day is lost
and I am tripping in a grocery store.

My father's career was decided on the simple fact that he was a butcher briefly and was therefore used to the sight of blood and so, "You're going to be a corpsman, son, for the United States Navy."

Months later, out in the bush, reduced from 220 pounds to 150 pounds in weeks, he learned that you don't stop to take a shit, you simply shit in your pants and keep moving.

And that was the easiest thing in Vietnam for him to get used to.

My mom was a Marine who volunteered for a tour of duty too. She collected what remained of wounded soldiers' brains and tried to mentally prepare them for their transition back to stateside.

Well, my parents survived, but at what cost?

They can't possibly be properly repaid.

This one is for my parents, both Vietnam Vets, having survived (somewhat) and having a proud son. Both of them doing enough tour duty (voluntarily) for me and my entire family forever.

Hearing the stories and living the life, I understand a room full of drunk and tearful Vietnam Vets as they all wail in unison, *"We've gotta get out of this place/ If it's the last thing we ever do."*

I give my parents long hugs when I see them.

And I continue to trip out whenever I see that homeless man still fighting for his life against those invisible VC.

Although, to him, I am sure they are quite real.

Dream #7093
(Spaghetti Head vs. the Ass Chairs)

I am sitting here suspending a string of spaghetti up above my tilted head. I slowly lower that strand until it circles the inside of my ear. I continue doing this, strand by strand, until I have filled my head with an entire plate of spaghetti.

Images of people making it in life cloud my mind as they come floating up into view.

I observe a number of stiff people clutching their wooden chairs to their asses with white knuckles as looks of terror streak across their faces. Each one floats up, sitting straight up, and then they trail off to either the left or right side of my view.

Images of people making it in life float up into view, pause there momentarily, and then slowly descend out of view.

Sometimes, there's an empty chair.

Sometimes, there's an empty chair with pieces removed where white knuckles once clutched.

I am sitting here and my hand is lowering strand after strand of spaghetti into my ear, while hundreds and hundreds of people clutch chairs to their asses in fear.

White Trash Theater

I am so drunk.

I am only catching bits and pieces
of everyone's conversation.

"We are now computerized," he apologized.

By the reaction on her face,
the apology was not enough.

"I'm not familiar with Natty Boh."

"I am red/green color blind."

"If your past boyfriend or girlfriend were a beer,
what would they be?"

I blurt out, "That's easy. Call me Rolling Rock."

And the novel unfolds, as we grab hold
of each and everyone's drinks and drain.

My friend tells a story about drinking
big tubs of interstate coffee on the way to Ocean City
and how he and his girlfriend were on vacation
and it was awesome.

And we exchange our first rock concerts:

"The Tubes."

"Led Zeppelin."

"Echo and the Bunnymen."

And something about someone being
a Christian Scientist until the age of 17,
and then the big dilemma –
Christ? Or alcohol?

And so drunkenness begins....

And now I'm under pins.

And everything just spins and spins and spins.

"By the way, those are hot suspenders
you are wearing."

I yell, "Get me another fucking Rolling Rock please.
I have some sins I need to appease."

I turn around and my friend is gone.

"Do you know where he lives?"

Everybody is having a great time
and I am just enjoying myself spitting on the walls
pretending to douse out the flames.

While someone else is getting paid a dollar
to create one.

The dollar is slid casually across the bar.

I spit on the flame
and spit drips down the lips.

And so it continues.

Heads nod to the music
and alcoholism continues.

Shedding of skin
and blood is drunk in large amounts.

Think about how often you wash your hair.

Rinse and repeat…
Rinse and repeat…
Rinse and repeat….

Killing Voices

Doesn't she ever shut up?

She walks through the door and immediately begins to shit through her mouth like some sick dog.

There must be something known as "Justifiable Homicide" in the law books somewhere.

"She wouldn't shut up, your Honor. And she was really stupid and annoying. I don't know, I just snapped and began choking her and I don't remember much else...."

Whenever I see her, to discourage conversation, I try not to make eye contact.

Like when that annoying man comes by to pick his orders up. I stare real hard at my computer and hope my phone rings so that I don't have to listen to his pathetic, puerile problems. But, it doesn't matter, he just goes on prattling to nobody, just to hear himself talk. Plus, he looks like a rat, small and rodent-like.

"Your Honor, he started rambling about how traffic was bad and how his back hurt and how he'd like to buy a new one and, before I knew it, I began choking him and I don't remember much else...."

There must be something in the law books somewhere regarding "Justifiable Homicide."

And if there isn't, there should be.

Some of the Best Words Were Never Spoken At All

Words.
Words are funny.

It seems that the more words that are put to paper,
the better.

It doesn't really matter what the words are,
just as long as more pages are filled.

Because, once the words stop,
death creeps in and settles.

Bukowski knew this, that motherfucker.

His pen stopped momentarily
while he took a rather long sip of beer.

He seized and fell out of his chair
before he could grab his pen up again.

He died there with his cheek against the wood,
cold.

And his limp dick lying against his left leg,
dead.

An unfinished poem dried on the page,
angered and betrayed.

And Bukowski lies dead
with horses running on his head.

Distracted

The ball skids across the table and misses.

I return to my stool feeling defeated.

My shoulders slump and my eyelids grow heavy. My eyes themselves, though, shift tirelessly from woman to woman to woman.

Some I want, some I don't.
Some, I don't.
Most of them, I don't.

Most brunettes, I do.
An occasional blonde or two.
No redheads to be seen.
I return to my brunette daydream.

The salesman I'm playing pool with couldn't sell his dick to a whore.

None of this makes sense because tonight is a weird night and I think I might be in love.

I will be getting a new television soon. And hopefully a new bed. And I can't decide if I'm a tit man or an ass man, because I appreciate a good either one or both.

I drink beer. And then coffee. And then water. And did I mention that I might be in love?

I sit there, feeling defeated, transfixed by all these women, but I'm distracted by something else.

And I'm quiet.

And…

"Oh, it's my turn?"

The ball skids across the table and misses again.

I shrug and return to my seat.

One Big Scratch

I don't want to fuck up...

I don't want to fuck up...

I don't want to fuck up...

I line up the shot for days.

And when I finally let the cue ball fly,
it glances off the eight ball and
falls into a pocket opposite.

The cue ball rattles around down below
and slams into the tomb of dead numbers
indicating yet another loss
for me.

"Fuck! My life is one big fucking scratch!"

She laughs, "You're so funny."

I rack another game of balls
and continue playing
despite.

I Am Not a Lush

I can taste
the dust on my tongue
as I drink from a green bottle
of homemade wine
that is very old.

I roll the fruit over my tongue
and down my throat.

Like resin to a bow,
the fruit leaves some residue on my tongue
that plays something harmonious when I
run it across the top of my mouth.

The poison burns
as it rolls down my throat
and forges a stone
in my stomach.

I tip the bottle again,
for the last time,
and sleep.

The Young Are Restless

They enter young still,
but their tricks are now old.

The first time they entered,
fresh, with new personalities.

Over time, those new personalities
became old, and then tired.

The same old tricks admired
are eventually expired.

Forever Behind the Times

Among the sneakers and Docs…
Among the bare feet and socks…

If only I could have been here before he got his hair cut,
I might know what the fuck is going on.

"Do you have like a before and after picture?"
As he tosses his new haircut about.

I feel so out of touch.
And seem to be only one day late.

Fuck.

And If You Finally Catch Your Tail, Then What?

Routines just seem to happen.
Nobody really looks for them.

You slip into them,
get used to them,

and then you don't know what to do
without them.

I've slipped into a few myself.

Pathetic.

Where's the Finish Line?

The young face wants to know, "How many
consecutive nights can one be fucked-up drunk?"

I tell him, "That's been done. For some, entire
lifetimes."

The question he should really be asking is,
"How many consecutive times can one be fucked-up
drunk in one night?"

That is one question I am still trying to answer.

I am up to four, and have been trying for five.

I climb the wall,
sleep at the top,
shift,
fall over the side,
and awaken on the other side.

I dust myself off
and begin again.

I dig my fingers into the lava slowly moving upwards
and catch a ride to the top.

I lie down,
sleep,
roll,
fall back over to the other side,
and awaken again.

I pick myself up
and start over.

Again…
and again…
and again.

Napkin Poem
(Near Closing Time and During)

Her large eyes look at me from beneath her red hair
and she doesn't know what to expect.

I just sold my seat, which was worth nothing,
for one dollar.

And I give my phone number away
on a Jack of Hearts Bicycle card.

I smoke four cigarettes, which I didn't buy,
and drink two free glasses of water.

I wear a scarf which is not mine.

I admire the artwork in the bathroom
by a girl named "Noodle"

as the Rolling Stones play on the speakers.

I underline shit in a novel that I don't understand
for a girl I don't know.

I write shit on this napkin.

A vacuum sucks up the dirt after closing.

The perfume from the scarf which is not mine
smells like a woman… a woman I want.

The vacuum gets passed over the bar
and trips up a stool.

That stool then gets placed upside down
atop the bar, at closing.

I am soon placed upside down
atop the bar, at closing.

And I don't know what to do.

The Rolling Stones roll their stones
on the speakers.

Vacuums vacuum.
Stools stool.

Five pennies lay on the bar, a forgotten tip,
which I gladly collect.

Waiting My Turn at Poetry Readings

"I wrote this poem while…"
"I wrote this poem while…"

"I wrote this poem while sitting in rush hour traffic…"

"I wrote this poem while listening to a song by Nirvana…"

"I wrote this poem while recovering from my self-inflicted wounds after a failed suicide attempt…"

"I wrote this poem while taking a tree bark bubble bath…"

"This poem was written when…"
"This poem was written when…"

"This poem was written when I was looking at my dead grandfather's face during his wake…"

"This poem was written when I was sitting on the beach drinking daiquiris…"

"This poem was written when I had my first sexual experience…"

"This poem was written when I was tripping out hard on acid…"

"This is a poem about…"
"This is a poem about…"

"This is a poem about all the cruel things that are being done to all the fishes…"

"This is a poem about everything cool regarding the 60s…"

"This is a poem about death and despair and human struggle…"

It's finally my turn.

I apologize, "I'm sorry, this is just a poem."

Cauliflower Ears

I stand here with a pain occurring
in the right front part of my brain.

Fortunately, I have the ability to convince
my brain that it does not belong to me.

I convince it that it belongs to the person
standing next to me.

I turn to that person and,

knowing their pain,
feeling their pain, and
sensing their pain,

I begin to beat about their sore spot with my fists,
hoping to deaden their pain into numbness.

I'm either successful
or I just made that pain a lot worse.

Leaving Her

It was inevitable, I guess.
The way it all went down.

She caught me in a lie and I admitted it.

She screamed, "You told a lie!"

I yelled back, "So fucking what!"

I had convinced myself that everyone in this world lies to someone at some time. This was my time.

She said, "It all comes back to you sometime."

She said this matter-of-factly, like she was speaking from experience.

She called me on the phone later and said, "I think we should break up."

I said, "Why?"

"Because you don't seem to be as into it as I am."

"Well, I would be *lying* if I disagreed with you."

And I don't think I emphasized the word *lying* in a smarmy way, but I might have.

"Okay."

"Okay, then."

"Good bye."

"Good bye."

For Her

I walk you to your car. I give you a hug.

You want more.

You say, "Am I going to get a kiss or what?"

I smile and say, "Of course."

It is all I have been wanting to do all evening. I didn't want to rush things. I like you too much.

I love your aggressiveness. More mature and assertive than anyone else I have ever met. You know what you want.

I lower my lips towards yours and kiss. Our tongues flirt and I can't help but gently bite on your lower lip with desire. I could bite on your lower lip for days and never grow tired.

You call me on the phone later. I am still woozy from our kissing and I tell you that I can't wait to get more.

You say, "Absence makes the heart grow fonder."

I say, "'Absence makes the heart grow fonder?' More like, 'Absence makes the desire much stronger.' Or, 'Absence makes the days seem longer.'"

The Ballad of Skip
(the gap-toothed one-eyed lacklip without a nose)

Born is a sometimes man
whose luck so bad
normal would never stand.

At age four or five, young naïve stared death in the eye.

A neighborhood dog gone bad
leapt from the porch on top of approaching innocence
and pulled his nose from his face with his teeth
and digested it.

Poor young man spent early days, and later days,
without a nose.

(The former seemed longer than the latter.)

One day in school, now third or fourth grade,
young noseless man sharpened his pencil
and to his desk returned.

He placed his pencil on his desk which rolled down the
desk, off the desk, hit the floor, and flipped up and over
until beneath the desk.

The young noseless man, his seat back pushed,
over stooped and under reached,
clutched pencil with sharpened end up in his fist,
lifted himself up, underbelly desk head struck,
a startled thrust down, a quick thrust up,
found young noseless man's eye on the end of his

pencil plucked.

The young noseless man, without one eye,
returned to his seat, pulled the eye from the end
and continued his work with one eye.

In early adolescence, one-eyed young one nose without
crossed the street and failed to see through his eyeless
socket that a car oncoming side blinded him.

The car random, in exact time and space exact,
smashed poor young eyeless one without a nose on the
knee direct and knocked that one leg dead.

Nerveless, and with little feeling, name now Skip,
he bobbed to momentum gain and swung
that dead leg around and forward.

And, sometimes, he put cigarettes out with his dead
leg's skin, just for his attention get.

Skip, now older, gained the attention of some woman
he thought he would never get.

And, for a time, he was happy.

With a woman never been, Skip so excited, and she so
willing, they both moved wild and cracked both heads
together in lovers' mis-undermoved switch.

Skip slammed his tooth into hers with some crazy kiss.
Skip's tooth lost, because it was chipped a half away.

They laughed at the bit of tooth displayed

in the palm of poor Skip's hand.

Skip tossed it aside and back to kissing they went.

The woman adored Skip's lips' kiss
and soon fell in love with his two untainted lips.

She proposed marriage, he hesitated,
they soon fell apart. She grew green with jealousy
that someone else might with Skip's lips kiss.

So, one night, in the dark,
she moved through Skip's sleep, felt over his face,
grabbed up his two lips with one hand and swiftly cut
them off with scissors in the other to preserve
Skip's lips' kiss for herself and no one else.

You can Skip still see
who throws his dead leg around
and through good eye leads.
A gap-toothed lacklip sight
whose teeth seem T-shirt white.
A moving testimony
that even noseless and without luck,
you can still get by,
and maybe still can fuck.

And through this black alternative reality,
a few missteps, a fraction of a second,
old Skip could very well have been me.

BLANK BOOK SEVEN

September – October

Another Renaissance

The birth of his death
the death of my birth

a star in the sky
an alcoholic illusion

Marat in his tub
Bukowski at the track

a muscle contraction
an inebriated delusion

simple scaled down
revolution

a rotation of space
a shifting face

a passing of time
and a changing of place

I find these lines much too constricting.

Piss puddle on the floor
hair drenched in whiskey
a bottle thrown against the wall
breaks.

I alone on stage

fumbling around
stumbling around
drunk
on stage.

A whiskey bottle
blue (or green)
a blue (or green) bottle
filled with whiskey
held loosely in my hand by the neck.

My drunk unpredictable motion
tosses my arm about
and the bottle is flung around
hanging at the end
of my arm's rope.

I teeter treacherously close
to the edge of the stage
and move back scared,
scared and afraid,
now angry.

I flip the bottle up in one motion
twirling the neck about
and empty the remaining whiskey
of the blue (or green) bottle
all over the stage.

I whip around in one violent motion
I snap my hand forward
and snap the bottle's neck free
and the blue (or green) bottle
shatters against the stage's back wall.

Blue (or green) pieces
scatter and settle at the base.

I twirl around wildly
my arms swinging behind
the motion of my body.

Wet whiskey hair
glazed red eyes
mouth poised rabid
chest heaving
I look out for a reaction
and wait.

Looking,
heaving,
and waiting.

Look Closer

beauty in tragedy
tragically beautiful
this poem will write itself forever

under angled light
small shadow reveals
the death of a teardrop
marking its spot

just below the young eye
that has already seen so much
sits the tiny indent
I love very much

nobody else has seen it but me
and I swim in it

so small, but I see it
like the sun sees the moon

I study it
I become one with it

I kiss it

I spread my kiss around it lightly
with my thumb

and then I kiss it again
slowly
softly

Dim Getting Dimmer

I smash a bug between my finger and the bottle
and I'm fucking bored.

I ate so much pasta that my heart just suddenly stopped.

I got it started again with a wine cooler
a couple hours later.

I think about whiting out every line in this book
because the order bores me.

Page after page of rose-colored lines
I just want the pages to be blank.

I want to fill the pages with my own lines.

I don't even want my words to be held
by these boring straight lines.

They're like prison bars on my brain
and I can't think straight.

Timeless Products

…your instructor flashes pictures of Greek fertility statues depicting women with hefty, dead breasts resting on their swollen bellies

but all you can see

are images of the top of my head buried between your legs in the back seat of your car late the night before…

"I have to go home," you gasped heavily,
but you were so worked up that you wanted more.

I lifted you off of me
and placed you in the corner of your car.

I undid your pants and started to remove your shoes,
but you said, "Leave the shoes on…"

I slid your pants down just below the knees
and lowered my head into the trap between your legs
and your pants and your cum.

I slowly caressed you with my tongue.

The slightest wrong move and my neck could have easily been snapped.

But that death seemed attractive,
I was not afraid.

We created beautiful art all evening, you and I,
first in being, a piece on canvas,
then in breathing,
and eventually in the back seat of your car.

Art came and then went
and then went and soon came...

and the only product was first put to canvas
and then fogged upon every window in your car.

My Dead Self

My dead self sits slumped in the chair
with a rather large, rather empty wine bottle
clutched loosely in my fist
while my head is thrown back resting on the chair.

The bass from the music slides around me,
between the walls and the floor and everything.

Like when, a moment before,
I curved that piece of paper in my hand
and slid it beneath that dead spider's back.

I was careful not to drop it,
while I moved towards the door.

Once through the door, I discarded it with a flick and
sent that dead spider flying dead through the air.

I closed the door and returned my shoe to its place.
I then returned to my boredom disgraced.

The bass slides beneath my dead self.
I am lifted and discarded.

I desperately clutch my rather large,
rather empty wine bottle.

Trying to Awaken the Muses

I bang my pen against the full, freshly-opened beer can
demanding that the spirits present themselves.

*"The scream of the butterfly
Come back [into my heart]"*

I am getting tired of hanging around
with my head on the table.

"What have they done to our fair sister?"

They have left her in the bushes,
the bushes of a world which rapes and cares not.

"So, when the [screaming's] over"

Blow out the candle
and listen to the music in the blackness.

"Come out! Come out! Come out,
you fucking motherfuckers!"

I bang my pen against the beer can
and demand that the spirits awake.

I demand that they present themselves
and either tear me apart or guide me.

I am ill and filled with the plague.
I want to know.

"Wake up! Wake up! Wake up,
you fucking bastards!"

I bang the can until it spits and then sputters,
but still… nothing.

"Fuck!"

I grab the beer up violently and drink
and then toss the can across the room.

It rattles against the wall
and rolls across the floor.

*"Take him by the hand
Make him understand"*

"The world on you depends"

But eventually it ends.

Like a long day,
descending deep
into the night.

Not For Sale

I lie in the cold grass, breathing.
Clouds pass quickly before the moon, like a dream.

We stand in line waiting for tickets to pass through the turnstile and be allowed a room for privacy.

This is a world run by a government that molds societies into Pavlovian routines.

Like a prisoner, I pass my days awaiting the next time I will get to see my lover.

Like prisoners, we pass our days at work awaiting the next time we get to see our lovers.

There is no talking in this dream, just motion and sight.

The day arrives, and with my lover, arm in arm, we move towards the ticket master, and we move towards the slow moving turnstile.

Once through, we feel free, a free not felt until we are through the turnstile.

We wander, arm in arm, and there is a structure to our left. It is dug and built into the ground and a window reveals to us a view from up above. We move a curtain aside from the outside and look through the window and down into an emptiness the size of an arena.

The outward appearance of the structure is deceiving. It appears much smaller than it actually is.

Down below pulse hundreds of lovers in various positions of disposition. Men savagely working from behind their women on all fours. Women with their heads thrown back and their arms thrown back as they ride their lovers' cocks. Circles of lovers connected in a massive display of oral sex. A wave of sexual motion in the vast well-lit emptiness of the arena.

We watch for a while and soon retreat to the privacy of a room where upon the floor we carefully lay a canvas and undress.

We kiss and dance about naked and soon begin to work on the canvas. We create beautiful art, swirling colors, divine figures, and emotions embodied on the lifeless fabric.

Hours pass and we soon collapse against a wall and smoke. We look at our art now propped up against the opposite wall. We look at each other and both nod.

I pack up some stuff, and our art, and I leave my lover naked against the wall of our rented room.

I sneak into a gallery across the grounds. I look around and scope out empty spaces for our love.

I scale a scaffold and sit high above and begin to take our art out of my pack, but I am discovered by the man appointed to the care of the gallery and he begs me to come down. I climb down, upset. He motions me to show him our love. I show him and his face becomes serious, and then soft. A tear appears, and he agrees to show our love in a space high and above.

Words are finally spoken in this dream…

He asks, "What is the price of this painted canvas?"

I reply, "There is no price. It is not for sale."

I quietly escape out the door alone, with a knowledge in my brain and a great weight resting on my heart, as I move back towards routine; thoughts of future days with my lover make my mind smile.

The gallery keeper places our love high up on the wall.

It is the only piece in the gallery on display without a price tag. Simply entitled,

"NOT FOR SALE."

Where is the Fucking Passion?

Nothing.
Nothing.
Nothing.

Have you ever watched the smoke dance
around the tip of a cigarette?

Have you ever understood the power in this?

Your words do nothing. They fucking escape one inch in front of your stupid mouth and die there. They don't even reach my ears. They die and fall to the ground, like an ash. An ash among many. Who cares?

Nobody.
Nobody.
Nobody.

I suck at a cigarette and a beer, hoping.
But, you provide me with nothing.

There is no passion.
There is no meaning.
There is no understanding.

Nothing.

I came here hoping to meet some like-minded poets, but I changed my mind, I am afraid to know any of you.

Have you never destroyed your brain
and collected it again?

Are you scared?

We are all scared.

I am scared.
But few can face it.

"Pussy!" "Wimp!" "Coward!" "Sucker!"

You've been it all.
We've been it all.
I have been it all.

It's all a joke to you. It's all a game.
No one really cares.

People clap anyway.
And always the worst prevails.

It's a joke, it's a game,
and no one cares.

That's the problem.
No passion.

Drunk Driving

We are all fish on this highway,
moving quickly past each other,
hoping we don't hit.

We sense the presence of one another
and move without touching.

I cling to the lanes,
staying between the lines
to remain alive.

I go screaming past an ambulance
and then suddenly decide to quit.

Because it just makes sense.

I snap free from the lanes
and go skidding across the norm.

I slam into the wall
and come slowly to a stop.

I am out.

And quickly,
the ambulance collects me.

I am a damaged fish removed from the school,
removed from the school of fish that conform.

Later, I drive drunk through a toad in the road

and pass an alien on the sidewalk.

I turn right past the bump
and park deadly on the night.

Stars stream piss across the sky,
the moon bounces like a fly.

I think, *What is it that makes us desire decadent foods?*

As I stumble quickly up the steep sidewalk
towards sleep.

The Absurdity and the Apocalypse

I wander through downtown with my young love in reach. We glide down streets as if in a dream.

On one of the streets, a parade commences.

Representations of different cultures and different countries and different countenances displayed. All marching (disguised) and dancing (hypnotized) behind speakers placed inside the backs of trucks that amble forward.

The scene is both wonderful and absurd as elegant female figures float with masks for faces, their identities concealed, never knowing who they are or who they were. Big bulbous constructions of eyes and large sharp-looking teeth.

I am so moved by the activity that I almost want to participate in the absurdity of this parade in the middle of downtown.

Instead, my young love and I turn down a side street that is blocked off by police.

I steer my young love from the sidewalk into the middle of the empty street, off our known path and towards a tunnel where no one else is.

The parade fades behind us as we enter the mouth.

I sense that this is the apocalypse…

Parades of forgotten cultures and somewhat remembered dances to somewhat forgotten tunes, heard, but no longer seen, behind us in the distance. A whisper. A reminder of what used to be.

We move through the silence and the wide-open emptiness; me and my young love attempting to fill the void with our smallness.

I run in circles and dance about wildly, throwing my arms in the air and hopping around, hoping to make myself seem larger than I really am. Hoping to fill the vast emptiness with my limitedness (and failing).

We exit the tunnel and make our ascent.

Met by a blockading police car, we return to the sidewalk and resume towards our destination.

Leaving the absurdity and the apocalypse, we return to the holocaust and look at past present futures.

Red Capricorn

You breathed Machiavelli back into my lungs
and brought him back into my heart.

You introduced Camus to my mind
and this was only just the start.

So begins the chronicle of a death foretold.

When given the choice between dismissing your sweet
lips kiss and sickness... I willingly took sickness and
was miserable for a week.

I would rather suffer an illness,
than be denied your lips.

We sit in the gallery
away from humanity
just you and I.

We drink coffee,
we smoke cigarettes,
and we engage in meaningful conversation,
while resting our bodies against oversized pillows.

We sit in the gallery and are confident that
one day soon these walls will be displaying our art.

This place which is our meeting place.
This place that started us being us.

Your mind challenging mine

your body challenging my mind
your being breathing and filling my being.

We have almost won.

We are almost one.

Free Dreaming I Naked of Everything Stop Sex

I want to get drunk and forget about my existence.

Just stumble through life oblivious to my actions
and without apology.

Bang into one wall,
bounce off of another wall,
I curse at all these fucking walls.

I fall flat on my face and pick myself up clumsily,
like a young fawn, and plod on.

Each time I fall, I achieve a higher level
of consciousness

as I contemplate the wet cold pavement
against my bloodless cheek.

And exhaling, with my hair in the wetness
on one side of my head.

And exhaling, with the backs of my hands
on the wet cold pavement beside me.

And exhaling, as the wetness soaks
through my clothing.

And at that moment of wet cold consciousness
realizing the absurdity and the beauty of falling on my
face drunk and wanting it to happen again and again.

Plodding on,
drunken stupid breathing,
bouncing off cursed walls,
and allowing my feet to trip over themselves
and cause my top heavy body to fall.

To give my face a moment upon the pavement to rest
and contemplate the reality of the absurdity.

Prolegomenon
(My Butt Sits Amongst the Rest)

I am stopped on the beltway, stuck in rush hour traffic.

I am smoking with my window open and Rage Against the Machine is blasting through my speakers.

I have my shoes off, my tie off, my left leg propped against the dash, one hand smoking, one hand driving, and one frustrated foot dancing from pedal to pedal, tapping out a distress signal to the universe.

I spend more time looking out my open window on the left, than I do looking at the bright brake lights in front of me. There's no point looking straight ahead. There's nothing happening, nothing moving.

I am pausing so long in this traffic that I am having conversations with people on the other side of the median strip traveling in the opposite direction. They are in the same situation as me.

Stop, and eventually go.
Stop, and eventually go.
Stop, and eventually go.

This guy yells over to me, "Hey!"

I say back, "Hey! How's it going?"

"Oh, I've been better."

"Yeah, me too. What do you think we can do about all this fucking traffic?"

"Oh, I don't know."

I suggest, "How about, starting next Monday, I go to your job and you go to mine? Because if you work near where I live, and I work near where you live, we should just trade jobs. Right?"

"Yeah, but I don't mind sitting in traffic, it means less time I have to spend with the wife."

"Is that the reason why there's all this traffic? A rush hour excuse for husbands not to be home?"

"Well, it's my excuse anyway."

"Maybe one day I'll relate to that, but I hope not."

"Yeah. Hey, we're moving. It was nice talking to you."

"Yeah, you too."

I lurch forward in traffic maybe four feet and then stop again.

I take a drag off my cigarette and then let my arm hang loosely out the window. I take one last drag and then toss the butt out the window.

I look down at all the discarded butts that are sitting there against the divider and I smile because I feel that I am contributing to some common goal. My butt falls short of the divider, rolls back and forth in the breeze still smoking, and is eventually slammed against the divider among the rest.

It exhales one last time and dies there.

Another motorist yells, "Hey!"

I say, "Hey! How's it going?"

"Oh, okay, I guess. Hey, the reason why your traffic is stopped is because there is an accident on our side of the road and everyone on your side is slowing down to take a look."

"Are you serious?"

He nods.

"Oh, fucking great!"

I hate this fucking place. Everyone's so fucking stupid.

I yank the steering wheel sharply to the left and accelerate right into the concrete divider.

I stop short of the wall, angry. I park my car and get out, angry. I plant my butt on the dividing wall with the rest of the butts and light up another cigarette.

I pull my legs up close to my body and plant my feet on the divider and smoke.

Startled by my action, the motorist asks, "What are you doing?"

"Quitting!"

"Why?"

"Because I'm tired of this shit! I'm tired of sharing the highway with a bunch of ambulance-chasing, spouse-avoiding, yellow-bellied bastards! I don't want to play anymore."

"So what are you going to do?"

"I don't know. I'm just going to sit here for a while and think. Either I'll hunker down here in protest to all this shit, or maybe I'll just wait for death. Death has to be preferable to this," I say, motioning to the traffic.

"All right, well, traffic's moving again, I gotta go."

"Yeah, see ya. Thanks for the shitty update."

He lurches forward about four feet and stops.

I start talking to everyone that stops there on both sides of the highway. Sometimes I converse with more than just one driver at a time.

It seems that my roadside protest is generating admiration from most, and disfavor from a few. Some people respect what I'm rallying against, others think I'm dumb.

Either way, I start some healthy discourse and bring attention to some much-needed topics. We need to end congested rush hour traffic and stop gawking at accidents. It's really pathetic. We're better than this.

The sun creeps down.

I end up talking to dozens of motorists from that divider and smoke a fraction of as many cigarettes.

But, I lie. I eventually get back in my car, move back into traffic, and go home.

I figure, another chance at failure
is a better option than quitting.

Shut Your Fucking Mouth

Some people cram large amounts of shit into their big stupid mouths which belong to their big stupid faces.

And they cram it in,
daily.

And then they puke all over us,
daily.

They puke on us with meaningless words puked from numb, empty minds that would rather surrender to a television sitcom than shut off the TV and challenge themselves or their brains.

Instead, they listen to mindless bullshit that some pathetic idiot put to paper.

Consider the fact that all sitcoms are products of things that were actually written down on paper.

Some asshole (or assholes) sat before some blank paper and puked their mind's concept onto it.

And we encourage them by tuning in.
And we encourage them by plugging in.

And we encourage them by shutting down our minds and slowly roasting our brains before the television.

We cram our heads full with bacon and French fries, coleslaw and Coke, milk and mustard and bread, and our stomachs and asses swell up in much anticipated flatulence.

I am tired of listening to entire populations
puking puke.

You can hear the cold fire fired up daily
and we don't even poke at it to stir or stoke it.

Just the simultaneous flipping of millions of television sets and the simultaneous creaking of millions of chairs and sofas as everyone's ass slips into the seat

and we cram more crap into empty heads, and puke in unison and move our asses aside to fart

while we sit numb before the prattling re-creation of the worst writing ever forced on paper.

Turn it off!
Turn it off!
Turn that fucking thing off!

(And sometimes silence is better, so
I'll just shut up.)

BLANK BOOK EIGHT

November – December

Are You Going to Save Me?

I stand, waiting my turn in an Asian-owned Laundromat.

My shoes are untied, most of my hair is falling out of my hat, and I haven't bathed since yesterday morning.

Behind me booms a voice, "Hey!"

"Yes?" I answer while turning around to see.

It's an older man with his gray hair slicked back, a red punch-beaten nose, and cheeks as pale as death.

He says, "I need to know where I can get a bottle of whiskey within walking distance."

I say, "I don't know if there is a place within walking distance. I know there is one further down that…"

He cuts me off, "Yeah, I know where that one is, I was hoping to get a bottle of whiskey here within walking distance."

"Sorry, I don't know of any other place."

I can't take my eyes off the wild whiskey desperation I see in his eyes as they flit about looking for an answer that's within walking distance.

"Well, I bet she doesn't even speak English," he nods, flipping his thumb at the storeowner. He turns and pushes his way through the door.

A shiver shoots straight up my spine.

I fear that I just met myself thirty years from now. Old and so desperate for another bottle of whiskey that I don't care who I ask.

Even if it is just eight o'clock in the morning.

Welcome to My Mind

In here, the spirits are uncorked
and subconsciousness reigns supreme.

Creativity and words fill my mind quickly.

The air in my head is thick
and the walls inside my skull drip with shit.

A white shirt would avoid bumping into those
saturated walls.

And kicking off one's shoes is not a consideration
for fear of what lurks beneath.

The spirits are drunk in and soon
creativity and poetry comes to pass.

Now, blind reckless abandon bubbles out of the
subconscious as the music gets turned up loud.

And, it's all over...

Bodies are thrown wildly about,
slamming into tables and chairs and walls.

A body is thrown back and forth over the partition, crashing into a table and cutting open the forehead, the back, the arm, and bruising the ass in the process.

The body breaks free and grabs up a bottle and rushes toward the window that separates the mind from the outside.

The bottle is smashed through the window
and both the bottle and the window shatter into pieces all over the sidewalk and street.

At this point, subconsciousness sees that a quiet party of consciousness is huddled around a table in a corner of the bar.

They are soon scared out of this place
as they move quickly out the door and away.

The reckless figure grabs up another bottle
and spills out onto the street after consciousness.

He flings the bottle at an adjacent building's face
and it shatters.

"Stay out! Don't come back!"

There is no room for order and reason in my mind.

The figure turns and stumbles back into Hell.

Now, even the bartender is getting into it,
throwing plastic cups and plastic ashtrays at the wildly dancing figures.

He's laughing and doesn't even care
that some of his business just got scared away.

The figures bump into each other drunk
and are filled with poetry.

Soon, the song ends and they collapse, exhausted.

Subconsciousness is triumphant.
Consciousness is scared and absent.

There are many spirits that fill this space which is my mind and is my own personal Hell embodied.

In the morning,
I wake up.

I look in the mirror and wonder how I cut that gash in my forehead. And then I wonder how I cut that gash in my arm. And then I wonder how I got that large cut on my back, which I discover while looking over the big bruise on my ass.

And I smile because I realize that each descent into Hell reveals new discovery and new understanding.

And all the scars and all the bruises
become lessons written into my body.

And I think, *Man, poetry is tough stuff.*

Warfare with My Fears

I, me
wish to be
bug-free.

I don't ask for much, I just want to be able to enter my bedroom and have some uninterrupted sleep.

But instead, I open the door and see one of them standing between me and my bed.

It's a cricket.

For some reason, my bedroom has become a portal for crickets, as they just started popping up all over my room. It's an infestation. They're pouring in from the walls somewhere.

Plus, they seem to sense any change in my room better than I can. Like when I've entered the room with intentions to kill.

I've fashioned a weapon out of a long slender box with a lid which once delivered a gift, but has now become a death-delivering extension of my arms for these crickets.

I used to box the bugs up and toss them outside unharmed. But I realized their numbers were too vast to continue engaging them in politicking and pleasantries.

Instead, I started gaining pleasure from tossing them into the toilet. But then I'd return to my room only to see that

I angered another one out of the woodwork.

With my sleep constantly delayed, I snap up each enemy and dispose of them, one by one.

Thoughts of them crawling on my face and shitting on my sleep is the only motivation I need.

To expedite the disposal process, I have moved the operation from my toilet to a bucket with water located closer to my room. I toss the POWs in the shallow water in hopes of staving off any more intruders.

This cricket standing between my bed and me manages to evade the box a couple times. And then, I get it, as the box crashes down around the cricket, and one side of the box separates a back leg from its body.

I scoop the dead leg into the box along with the body, and toss both into the bucket alongside another POW that is floating there dead.

The five-legged bug starts a freakish swim in circles with its uneven distribution of appendages. It side strokes around the corpse of the other and occasionally bumps into its own dead leg that is floating.

I am exhausted. I retreat to my bed and sleep.

I dream of confrontations with my fears and my dreaming is taut with stress as I run from oversized bugs that are chasing me.

At one point in my dream, a spider leaps from my sleeve,

lands in my bellybutton, and bites.

I smash the spider with my finger and pick the spider parts out of my bellybutton in pieces.

Two spots of blood leak out of my bellybutton.

I awaken from my dreaming screaming.

I consider the irony and the absurdity of my dreams and laugh.

I get up and move towards the bathroom to piss.

I peer into the bucket at the now water-bloated lifeless two bodies and the one still-floating dead leg among some dirt and a spent cigarette butt and…

all is dead and silent and still
in that piss-colored broth.

I spit into the bucket.

I, me
wish to be
bug-free.

Faces and Facades

Malls are madhouses.

Faces of the sad and the important rush around
and in and out of black-bordered storefront facades
filled with fancy displays of their goods.

And I sit on a bench with a French fry
and watch absurdity rush by.

Women in tight tops are being led around by their clearly visible erect nipples in the air-conditioned coolness. Most are walking with a man in hand or alone.

People from various pasts move past.

Children cling to their mothers
or are pushed by their fathers.

In the food court, people shuffle through lines with food on their trays, hungry and mad. They bump and push so that they can more quickly get to cramming their fat empty heads with food from the cafeteria, satiating their already swollen bellies when they should be satiating their fat empty heads instead.

Store managers rush by me with their keys wound up around their arms like armbands, like some badge or medal, and act like, "Look at me rush around! I am so important! Do this! Do that! Do This! Do that! Sieg Heil! Sieg Heil! Sieg Heil!" as they rush by acting so important and special.

And I share a bench with a French fry.

A man sits down next to me and his wife wants to squeeze in between us. She tries to remove the French fry by swatting at it.

She swats and she swats and then *swat*!
She sends that French fry sailing right into my shoe.

And I think, *You dumb stupid bitch*, and shoot her a look that communicates the same.

All she says is, "Oops!" as she swings her big stupid Steak Escape ass around and sits and rests her big Taco Bell belly right where the French fry once lay.

Fear shoots up my spine as from behind I thought I saw my ex-girlfriend now grown to a ten-foot height and two hundred pounds heavier, looking angry and ready to kick my ass dead.

Lovers pause at jewelry in the window.

The rats scurry about with their hands full of desperate disregard and an urgency of descending winter
and holidays.

Bits of conversation slip into my ear,

"In my country…" a woman explains to a man.

And,

"I think she is having surgery next week…" says a

mother to her daughter.

And,

"Want to get some ice cream?" a woman asks her three children.

And,
malls are truly madhouses.

Stinking of insanity and mental instability constantly demonstrated through the absurd routines of people in malls everywhere, and scarred across the faces of the lame who rush around with false self-importance.

And now, I am looking at the French fry smashed on the ground, flattened by a fleeting foot.

And now, slowly,
I am going mad.

Happy Birthday

uncooked spaghetti is sprung from the box by unsteady hands and hits the floor like pick-up sticks.

his wife's neck quickly snaps, her eyes narrow and lips purse as she silently stabs him twenty times quickly with a knife in her mind.

the knife is returned to its sheath almost as quickly as the neck is snapped and the wounds are administered.

cables tighten around the son and suddenly bloodbaths become desirous in the silence.

each strand of uncooked spaghetti is picked up one by one by the careless husband and the son.

the husband suffers from multiple stab wounds and the son has already been killed a thousand times before.

the cables tighten and the spaghetti is tossed into the boiling pot and cooked.

Silence beneath the Bedpost

Vodka, Scotch, and whiskey.

The unbearable baby screams, "Why? Why does my butt not inflate?"

As if sensing the larger catastrophe in all things living, the baby wants to inflate its butt and float away.

I meet Bob, and Doug, and God in here tonight.
We talk about the Bible, about the cold, about infection.

I am awaiting the cold realism
of alcoholism and sex.

Barflies occupy the stools
and talk shit.

A twenty-dollar bill is removed, and then elevated
above the head for the bartender to see.

Twenty-dollar bills pay for stuff.

My Adidas foot rests on the chair,
waiting to insert itself into a pussy.

Slowly it will be slid into the slit.
First the tip, and then the foot.

Stomping into deaf caverns and orgasms,
denied.

"Hi," she says.

"Hello," he replies.

She can't stay away.

He says, "That'll be three dollars."

She asks, "Don't you remember me, John?"

"No, I don't."

The knife is slid slightly deeper into her side.

The shelves hold nothing but dust and the scars of lit cigarettes once left there before.

Cue balls are forced into experience.

White, and soon thrust in different directions, forced to interact with other numbers.

"Would you here hold my hand?
Would you here hold my heart?"

Her dress was once white, now it's all red.

My cigarette bends its own death.

Good Fucks and Bad Fucks

He hasn't been with a good fuck in two years.
But he was with a bad fuck a month ago.

He describes how he jumped out of bed, pointed at her,
and said, "You, are a bad fuck."

His dick got stuck in his fly on the way out the door.

During the drive home, he began to cry.

He was glad he didn't drive a stick shift,
his crying became that uncontrollable.

Just then, across the bar, an angry man in a torn sweater
erupts. Everyone is upset at the tipless, torn-sweater man
for interrupting.

Shots are drained.

Cigarettes are smoked.

Pool is played and some tempers inflamed.

Smiles and laughter fill the room as the holidays fill more
cups and soak the paper towels with piss.

Bangs hide the faces that reek of ripened realities.

And soon the spanking begins.

I pose this question, "Would you kill somebody if you knew you could get away with it?"

The man in the torn sweater, which is now off, is completely drunk as he is reluctantly led down the stairs. He throws a wild fist at the exit sign which then spins there by a wire.

The bouncer throws the torn sweater out into the street. And the tipless drunk man starts laughing.

That laugh.

That fucking obnoxious laugh.

But, our attentions again are brought back.

He says to me, "You seem so familiar. I feel like I have known you for years," as the familiarity of a fellow man comfortable in bars brings camaraderie.

He continues, "God damn, it's nice to meet you. Here, have another drink."

His hand claps my shoulder
and then his eyes narrow.

He asks me, very seriously, "You laid into any good pussy lately?"

I say, "Well, the last one begged me to spank her, so I spanked her until my hand hurt, and I stopped after a while because it was no longer fun."

"Who was on top?"

"We both were."

"Awesome. Now that's a good fuck!"

Barroom Brawling

Have another drink, you stupid asshole,
you stupid motherfucker, have another drink.

You are so stupid.

How did I end up sharing the same space with you?

You want to get bloody over a quarter you misplaced,
and then accused others of stealing.

Have another drink, you son of a bitch.
Have another.

You ain't getting pussy tonight,
because there ain't no pussy to be got.

So, have another drink
and fight.

Punch Drunk and Without Bail

Sobriety is painful, honest thoughts remind me,
and my hair continues to grow over my eyes.

Broken glass collects at the bottom of the can
and I'm still half a man, but mostly a child.

I think, *Fuck this!*

I open my mouth and exhale.
I try to speak, but no words come out, only fists.

People point their fingers at a mother's spread legs;
they've cornered her in the alleyway.

Nobody remembers her face. Her face falls into shadow and now only her exposed pussy lays splayed and displayed before their pointing fingers. The fingers move into the spotlight and poke at her bloody pussy.

The mother's sobbing is drowned out
by their angry cries.

They don't see her face,
they only see her legs spread.

Fingers close into fists and begin beating about the mother's body. She closes her legs and tries to defend herself.

I am a cold witness to this and I wish for a beer.

Sobriety is painful, honest thoughts remind me, and my hair continues to grow over my eyes.

A fist lashes out and strikes the mother in the mouth. Blood discolors her teeth and drips from the corner of her mouth, down her chin.

I lower my head and shuffle away.

I move out of the alley and into a bar. I grab a stool and my body becomes a heavy weight as the burden of knowledge lowers my head and weakens my will.

The bartender slides towards me, "Yeah?"

"Three shots of anything, and a pitcher to chase them down with."

The shots go down fast.

The clumsy bartender spills half my beer in front of me. In one motion, I throw my head back and then forward, flipping all of my hair into the puddle of beer before me. I mop up all the spilled beer with my hair and smooth my wet hair back with my hands.

I begin working on the remainder of the pitcher and, suddenly, with the hair out of my eyes, I can see clearly again. It's just that now, I'm drunk again. Things make sense in this state.

Friends blur out of view as time pushes them further away.

I spit at the me in the mirror and curse my black being.

My inability to communicate blurs my friends into dots on my drunken horizon. I try to knock one of them down with a stone, but time has put too much distance between us.

I sit on my stool and watch time put more distance between me and them.

Beer remains within reach and I drink to make time and distances seem less important.

My spit dries on the mirror and my curses only resound in my head.

My hair dries slowly and, piece by piece, my hair falls back over my eyes.

The bartender slides over towards me and tells me he has to close.

I move back out into reality and fists begin falling out of my mouth. I try to hold them in with my hands, but I can't hold back the flow of fists I am now puking out of my head. They come out of me in torrents, and soon the disembodied fists just lie there dead on the sidewalk.

I wipe my tired mouth with my sleeve and curse my inability to communicate.

Time and distance continues to die unheard.

I shuffle towards the cold reality of bullshit and think about my next beer.

The masses have cornered another pussy in the alley and the prosecution begins.

They raise their arms and extend their fingers to point and prod at the new pussy now splayed and displayed at the end of the alley.

The shadow moves over her face
and the crowd moves in for a closer look.

They want the pussy to spread its legs wider.

Each time the legs are spread, inch by inch,
the heads move in for closer inspection.

The body can feel the breathing of a million heads craning their necks, as they examine her as closely as possible. The heads actually pass into the pussy and the legs are nearly broken as they're spread much further than they're meant to be.

Eyes look over the walls inside the pussy.
Lips are licked.

Millions of eyes slowly close and millions of tongues are extended as they long to taste the inside of this pussy.

But, the legs snap shut, and millions of heads are abruptly aborted.

They become enraged.

Fingers close into fists once again
and they begin showering the body with blows,

again and again,
over and over,

until there is nothing left but the collective motion of a
bored people looking for another pussy to bloody.

Broken glass continues to collect in the can.
And my hair continues to grow.

Honest thoughts stab me,
because sobriety is much too painful to bear.

What Am I?

I am pain. I am death.

I am comfortable in the corner, in the shadow, with my legs pulled tight to my chest.

I am coward.
I tremble in the darkness at my power.

Only the whites of my eyes can be seen in the darkness.

Too many times I have moved into the light, out of my corner, and caused pain, and sometimes death.

Too many times I have reached out to another with my finger and felt their warm skin beneath it and then felt my finger turn their skin ice-cold.

I drain them of life and then demand more.

They say, "Fuck you!"

And I say, "Fuck you back!"

And they say, "Fuck you further!"

And I say, "No, fuck you, you're dead."

And I move back into my corner, a coward,
and pull my legs up close for protection.

The problems occur when I begin to relax,

when I begin to feel comfortable.

I loosen my legs from my grasp, lift myself up, move into the light, and soon another victim passes.

I don't look for them, I create them.

And then, I kill them.

I create them with my mind.
I mold them and shape them.

And, for a time, I am happy.

But then, I touch them with my finger and it's just a matter of time before I drain the life out of them through the spot where my finger touches.

I remove my finger and they crumble away.

I don't have enough patience to kneel down and collect them in my arms, so, I turn my back on their death and move into the corner and, like a coward, I slide down the wall and into a ball.

The only thing I collect in my arms are my legs clutched close to my chest.

I tremble in the darkness, with only the whites of my eyes discernible in the shadow.

In a World of Shit

Flush.

Down and around
watch the motion with your eyes.

Breathe.

Around, around, around,
and then down.

Feel the weight of your stomach
on top of your intestine.

Bile, diseased, and distended,
it expands in your middle.

And then, pain.

You unbuckle your pants,
but the pain remains.

A child remembers long into adulthood the image of a friend bending over his bare ass before him, spreading his ass cheeks wide with both hands, and revealing a shit ring from an unwiped ass.

A lesson from the world in a tiny childhood bathroom memory.

A friend takes a shit, lifts himself from the bowl, laughs at his idea, turns around, bends down, and spreads his dirty asshole wide with both hands and laughs.

The world never stops showing me its filthy ass.

Friends become enemies,
enemies become preferable,

and soon…

Flush.

Down and around
watch the motion with your eyes.

And breathe,

because it's the only thing
you can do.

(Author Photograph by Chris Maroulakos)

About the Author

Greg Gerding was born in Fort Thomas, Kentucky, on May 12, 1971. Gerding is the only child of a career Navy father and a Marine mother, both of whom volunteered for service at the height of the Vietnam conflict and did tours of duty in Vietnam during the war. By the time Gerding turned 18, he and his family had moved 15 times, landing in Kentucky, Virginia, Ohio, Pennsylvania, California, Illinois, and Maryland.

In 1994, the year *Loser Makes Good* was written, Gerding had just earned his degree in English from the University of Maryland and was working various jobs throughout the D.C. area, first in retail and then with a company that supplied industrial air filtration products. Over the course of that year, he broke off a relationship that was leading to marriage, moved out of the place he shared with her in Bethesda, Maryland, moved into a roommate situation in Fairfax, Virginia, and moved again into another roommate situation in Rockville, Maryland.

Gerding read a magazine article featuring an interview with Henry Rollins which turned him on to the poetry of Charles Bukowski and further inspired him to write and read his own work at poetry venues around D.C. Frustrated by the limitations placed on artists at such venues, Gerding started a weekly reading series at his favorite bar, *Hell*. He organized and hosted *Poetry in Hell* for two years, and made sure there were no rules.

Loser Makes Good is Gerding's first book.

CPSIA information can be obtained at www.ICGtesting.com
Printed in the USA
LVOW052158220712

291025LV00003B/7/P